The Billingsgate Market Cookbook

CJ Jackson

The Billingsgate Market Cookbook

CJ Jackson

First published in 2009 by New Holland Publishers (UK) Ltd
London • Cape Town • Sydney • Auckland

Garfield House
86–88 Edgware Rd
London W2 2EA
United Kingdom

80 McKenzie Street
Cape Town 8001
South Africa

Unit 1
66 Gibbes Street
Chatswood
NSW 2067
Australia

218 Lake Road
Northcote
Auckland
New Zealand

ISBN 978 1 84773 547 8

Commissioning Editor: Emma Pattison
Designer: Jason Hopper at District-6
Photographers: Myles New and Lis Parsons
Food stylists: CJ Jackson, Monaz Dumasia,
    Eithne Neame and Frances McKellar
Props stylists: Rachel Jukes
Production: Laurence Poos
Editorial Direction: Rosemary Wilkinson

10 9 8 7 6 5 4 3 2 1

Reproduction by PDQ Digital Media Solutions Ltd., United Kingdom
Printed and bound in Singapore by Tien Wah Press (PTE.) Ltd.

Contents

Introduction

A London Institution

If you live anywhere near London and eat fish then chances are you've tucked into a meal whose key ingredient originated in Billingsgate Market. From fishmongers to fish and chip shops, famous restaurants to local takeaways, all manner of eateries rely on the largest inland fish market in the United Kingdom for their supplies of fish and shellfish. With somewhere in the region of 25,000 tonnes of fish and fish products changing hands in the market every year, Billingsgate is a hub of commercial activity. However, it's not just the fish that lends Billingsgate its success and status. Like any established market Billingsgate is more than simply a sum of its parts. While the fish keeps the market traders in business and the customers coming back, the market itself is a heady mix of history, pride, hard work, tradition and camaraderie.

The Hidden Gem

Situated in the heart of London's Docklands, the frenetic pace and historical kudos of the market are more than a match for the financial institutions that surround it. Although the unassuming building sits squatly in the shadows of its impressive high-rise neighbours, the bland façade only serves to belie what's going on inside. Here, shirts and ties are swapped for Wellington boots and aprons, and city lingo takes a back seat to market banter.

The Billingsgate Experience

Anyone who makes the effort to set the alarm clock and head down to Billingsgate to buy their fish is rewarded not just by the fantastic selection and quality of what's on sale but also the rich experience of hands-on shopping. In a culture that has become dominated by shrink-wrapped micro morsels, it's genuinely refreshing to be able to smell, touch and choose your food. From the incredibly beautiful to the downright ugly, a fish should be viewed as more than a collection of uniform squares in a polystyrene tray. It's also far easier to check for quality and freshness if you're looking at the whole fish. However, this connection with real food is something that alienates many people. Most of us have been raised on the supermarket phenomenon and find it daunting to be brought face-to-face with our food in a more natural state. Billingsgate offers the ideal opportunity to get closer to the source of our food and to partake in a centuries-old tradition in this centuries-old institution.

Billingsgate is a heady mix of history, pride, hard work, tradition and camaraderie

BILLINGSGATE MARKET
Loch DUART Ltd
The Sustainable Salmon Company
Scottish Sea Farms

A Word from
CJJackson

After three years as Director of the Seafood Training School, I am still excited by working at Billingsgate market. The wonderful array of fish on offer, and the buzz and atmosphere on the market floor in the early hours of the morning is something that has to really be experienced to be appreciated.

The Billingsgate Seafood Training School

The school is situated on the first floor of the market. As a charity the focus is on teaching children about the enjoyment and benefits of eating fish as part of a healthy diet. We aim to support the market by delivering industry-related courses for potential fishmongers, and also offer courses for those seeking to increase their knowledge of seafood, from quality assessment courses through to sustainability seminars.

We receive support from the Billingsgate merchants, The City of London and importantly The Worshipful Company of Fishmongers' and their fisheries staff. As a charity we also benefit from the financial support of The Sir John Cass's Foundation, Aldgate and Allhallows Barking Exhibition Foundation and the Isle of Dogs Community Foundation. Some of our charitable activity is supported by money generated from fee-paying courses delivered to the general public. These enthusiastic cooks want to enjoy more fish and are keen to learn how to recognize quality when buying seafood as well as the preparation and cooking of different species.

Sourcing Fish Responsibly

At the school we aim to work with and handle responsibly sourced and sustainable species and talk openly to our guests about the many different issues surrounding all types of seafood. Fish is seasonal and we try to avoid working with species of fish when they are heavily in roe or just after spawning when they are not at their best. We focus on the positive stories about sustainability and believe that, in an often-negative environment, the good news stories should be celebrated and shared.

The sustainability of all seafood is an extremely complex and emotive subject and there are many stories to tell. British-landed fish sold at Billingsgate is always fished legally to quota and, in many cases, is subject to a minimum landing size, ensuring that the species have a chance to breed. The quotas are set by the European Commission and are based on information gathered through constant scientific research. The seas around our own coast are carefully monitored and the information gathered there enables an informed decision to be made regarding key stocks of fish. What makes matters more complicated still is that the story on each species of fish changes with the seasons.

Attending a Course

People attending courses often admit to having a limited repertoire of fish dishes and want to learn more; they may understand the benefits of eating seafood but are often put off by not knowing what to choose or how to prepare it, and importantly how to cook it well. Many don't have access to a good fishmonger and are disillusioned by the lack of experience and knowledge of some of the major retailers. They also do not have access to the huge range of species that are available at Billingsgate and therefore simply don't try new things. With this in mind the better-known species of fish are rarely used at the school, and instead we aim to work as much as possible with under-utilized species and those that may be less familiar to our visitors.

The atmosphere on the market floor in the early hours of the morning is something that really has to be experienced to be appreciated

There is a huge range of seafood available at the market and there can be up to 150 species of fish and shellfish on a good day trading. There are some great alternatives to the better-known fish and by encouraging people to be brave, change their eating habits and trying something different, we hope to expand their understanding, knowledge and enjoyment.

The Ultimate Fast Food

We have our own ethos about cooking fish and this is reflected in the recipes in this book. We see fish as the ultimate fast food. The focus of our courses is always on the fish and its preparation and as we have access to some of the freshest fish available in the UK, we aim to keep the recipes quick and easy. Methods of cooking such as pan-frying, baking, roasting and grilling with simple flavours rarely fail to please. Few of these recipes will take more than thirty minutes to cook.

Buying Fish at Billingsgate

What makes a trip to Billingsgate so refreshing is that the merchants have a very in-depth knowledge about the products they are selling; many of them have worked on the market all their lives and have lived through the many changes seen at the market over the last few decades. They deal with the seafood first hand and are able to provide information as to how a fish has been caught, where it came from and in many cases what boat actually landed it. Often they will also be able to offer information on how to store and cook a product. Similarly fishmongers who buy wholesale from the market will also have access to this information.

Changing the buying habits of a lifetime means that we can benefit from so many different fish and with this in mind it is quite possible to not eat the same fish more than once every so often. We also find that as a nation today we are so used to seeing seafood in a ready-prepared state – no bones, skin or heads – that many of our guests have no idea what many of the fish they may enjoy actually look like. This is one of the reasons why a market such as Billingsgate is an exciting, visual place to visit. As this book only focuses on a selection of the key species that are prepared and cooked at the school, a trip to Billingsgate to see what else is on offer is a must.

Cooking Fish

The species selected in this book simply provide an overview of the fantastic selection of species on offer and if this encourages the reader to try something new for a change (and enjoy it) it will have succeeded to spread the good news story. We see a recipe as a starting point and not a destination so although the recipes utilize these species, in some cases we leave the choice open for the cook to adapt the recipe to their own tastes.

For further information regarding what seafood to choose for your recipes there are various websites that might prove helpful: The Shellfish Association of Great Britain, Seafish, The Marine Stewardship Council, Seafood Choices Alliance and the Marine Conservation Society among others. These groups publish up-to-date information about many species of seafood that are not just available at Billingsgate market, but all around the UK.

The sea provides us with a bountiful resource and countless varieties of seafood that all have their own unique flavour and taste. Hopefully this book will inspire the reader to broaden their outlook and try some of these different species.

CJ Jackson, Director,
Billingsgate Seafood Training School

The History of
Billingsgate

Origins

Billingsgate market is so steeped in history that its origins can be traced all the way back to Roman times. However, details of this period are fairly sketchy and the first major historical reference to the famous market was in 1327. Edward III was King of England at the time and it was his charter that gave markets in the City of London exclusive trading rights. No other markets were allowed within a 6.6-mile radius of the City and this ensured the future of Billingsgate, along with Smithfield and Cheapside. Although this might seem like a figure plucked at random by a bored clerk it was actually a carefully calculated number. It was believed to be the greatest distance that someone would be able to walk to a market, set up a stall, sell their wares and then walk back home afterwards – all in the space of a day. Whether or not they collapsed from over exertion once they arrived home was another matter.

The Name Game

Plenty of people have had plenty to say about Billingsgate over the years and the origin of its name is no exception. There are a couple of theories as to how and why the market got its name and, as with many places that stretch so far back in history, we can only hazard a guess at the truth and may never really know the answer. One school of thought links the name to a Celtic King called Belin who ruled around 400BC. At the time London was still in its infancy and was no more than a paltry collection of mud huts. Belin obviously felt these huts had potential as he arranged for a wall to be built around them and cut out a space on the

A customer at Old Billingsgate, sensibly dressed in wellington boots, barters with a merchant.

riverfront to allow boats to land. In some ways it's a bit of a stretch of the imagination to link this ancient King to the naming of the market but it's a romantic story and there is a definite connection to the river. Other, less speculative theories have the name being derived from a landowner a little later on in history. What is known is that the market was referred to as Blynesgate and Byllynsgate before the present name was adopted.

From Coal to Cod

Billingsgate is such a London icon in terms of its culinary, cultural and historical value that it seems hard to believe that it was never intended to operate solely as a fish market. The original market was located on Lower Thames Street and it was the misfortune of Queenhithe – a port further upstream – that allowed Billingsgate to steal the piscatorial limelight. Queenhithe traditionally took delivery of most of the fish coming into London, leaving Billingsgate to scrabble around for the leftovers. Ships would generally only dock there when there wasn't any more space at Queenhithe. However, as cargo ships grew bigger they couldn't physically navigate under Old London Bridge and it made sense to start unloading cargo downstream at Billingsgate. Although it always sold fish, in its early days customers at Billingsgate could also buy everything from pottery to coal. However, the demise of Queenhithe tipped the scales and fish became big business at Billingsgate. The City of London and the Fishmongers' Company encouraged the growth of the market, as it meant that the sale of fish would become more centralised and easier to oversee. But it wasn't until sometime in the sixteenth century that it became widely known as a fish market and it became the hub of the London fish trade. In 1699 things became official when an Act of Parliament decreed that it was 'a free and open market for all sorts of fish whatsoever'. In a little quirk to this law, an exception was made to the Dutch fishermen who moored in the Thames. As a 'thank you' for their help in keeping Londoners in fish during the Great Fire they were given the exclusive rights to sell eels. Trade had to take place from their boats so presumably customers who were prone to seasickness would have taken eel off the menu.

A Plaice to Call Home

Over the years, other smaller fish markets came and went. Merchants saw the opportunities on offer at Billingsgate and desperately tried to claw away some of the increasingly lucrative fish trade for themselves. However, they tended to only make a brief appearance on the market scene before bowing down to the superior reputation of Billingsgate. The market continued to flourish in terms of traders, stock, customers and reputation and the original site on Lower Thames Street began to strain with the ever-increasing traffic of people and vehicles. Situated on the north side of the Thames, between London Bridge and Tower Bridge, it was ideally located for deliveries from ships on the riverfront and carts from the road. But in terms of trading it was a pretty haphazard affair with makeshift stalls hustling for space close to the riverfront. Incredibly, there was no formal market hall until 1850, when the first market building was constructed. After hundreds of years the merchants finally had a formal space in which to sell their wares and have a bit of protection from the weather.

It wasn't exactly an enduring legacy for the great market: the building only lasted 23 years before it was torn down to make way for something more practical and imposing. The new building, designed by Sir Horace Jones, fared a little better and it was home to the market until it moved to the Isle of Dogs in 1982. Compared to the pretty basic amenities of the previous building, the new market hall was a veritable showcase of mod cons. Steam powered the lifts and boilers and the merchants had a bit more space to spread out their displays. There was also space for shops and offices and plenty of room for customers to mill about and take their time choosing their dinner. However, the new building didn't completely transform Billingsgate – much of the character and many of the characters of the old market remained.

Fish Wives and Fisticuffs

Throughout history fish markets have been associated with some less than salubrious activities and behaviour at Billingsgate was

no exception. The ubiquitous 'fish wives' loitering in the entrance to the market, the tendency to solve disputes with a couple of rounds of bare knuckle fighting and the liberal use of expletives in daily banter are just some of the examples of why the market had a dubious reputation. It is certainly true that the London markets tended to attract a motley crew of colourful characters. Equally, it's easy to see why a merchant or porter needed to have their wits about them and be able to handle themselves in sticky situations. Unsociable hours and unsavoury working conditions are bound to toughen a person up and this was no job for the fainthearted.

Pickpockets thrived in the busy market setting, whilst the local taverns attracted a raggedy bunch of hardened sailors, seasoned drinkers and petty criminals. It was no place for a lady, which would go some way to excusing the fearsome reputation of the fish wives, whose language was only matched by their bawdy behaviour. In fact, the women were so renowned for their vociferous cursing that the word 'Billingsgate' was adopted into everyday speech and literally meant 'foul language'. Although this hotbed of raised voices and animated tempers would have been shocking to an outsider, much of the banter between the merchants, porters and buyers was good-humoured. The very nature of market life would have demanded a fine pair of lungs and a varied vocabulary. If you couldn't make yourself heard over the general din, or you couldn't argue your point when it came to buying or selling fish, then you probably didn't have a promising future at Billingsgate. Quick wits and a quick humour are traits that have been inherited by the merchants and porters at Billingsgate today and you'll probably still hear words that would make a vicar blush.

All Change

Although daily market life, with its routine and hierarchy, remained pretty much the same over the years, the way in which fish was caught, bought, delivered and sold changed dramatically. Today,

CLOCKWISE FROM TOP LEFT: Mr Watkin, a former Chief Inspector of The Worshipful Company of Fishmongers, inspects a lobster with an official carapace measure; the premises of A. H. Cox, established in 1862; porters taking a break under the market's Lower Thames Street arcades; a pause for breath in the hot, steamy atmosphere of the Boiling Shop; porters wheeling their steel-shod trollies over the cobbled streets of London; the boiling of shellfish – an essential service offered by the market.

a merchant might sell anything up to 30 different varieties of fish on his stand. However, back in the eighteenth century, people popping down to Billingsgate to buy their supper would only have had about 20 varieties to choose from in the whole market and most of these would have been caught in and around the Thames. Bygone customers would have been blissfully unaware of the effects that the media, international travel, ethnic diversity and transportation methods would have on the fish trade over the next hundred or so years and the sheer variety of fish available now is due to all of these factors. Whilst native fish are still very much a part of the market – and indeed many are enjoying a renaissance – we are now able to try fish from all over the world.

As the fish have adapted to international travel so the transportation methods have adapted to the growing demands of the clientele. Once upon a time, everything arrived at Billingsgate by boat. It seems obvious that a fish market located on the riverfront would have its fish delivered by boat but Londoners had a voracious appetite for aquatic vertebrates and demand began to exceed supply. As fishermen ventured further afield, in search of bigger catches, the landlubbers gathered together to devise ways of transporting the fish to market quickly and efficiently. Whilst boats could take a catch so far, you could never rely on the British weather and even a slight delay could spoil the cargo. The answer was found on the railways and by the late eighteenth century most of the fish arriving at Billingsgate had travelled by train from ports all over the country. Kings Cross was the major London destination and the fragile cargo was greeted by horse-drawn carts, ready to take it on the last part of the journey. This set-up seemed to be pretty successful and railways continued to do much of the major transportation for the next hundred years.

That is until the long distance lorry driver packed up a flask and sandwiches, tuned in the radio and prepared to give the railways a bit of competition. It didn't take long for the accountants to do their sums and work out that the motorway was the way forward for fish. Lorries could pick up the cargo directly from the ports and deliver it to the market door. The fish was handled less and was transported the whole way in a refrigerated environment so it arrived fresher and was more likely to be intact. In little over a decade, lorries had swooped in and taken on most of the fish transportation. You can't stop modernisation and these

The old premises of C.J. Newnes and Partners, who still trade at Billingsgate today.

advancements in transportation were absolutely crucial to the survival of the market and its ability to supply London with fish. However, when making the transition from sea to road, via the railways, Billingsgate unwittingly set the wheels in motion for its demise on Lower Thames Street.

Market on the Move

Whilst the merchants and porters continued to bustle about inside as they had for hundreds of years, the sounds of construction echoed all around the outside of the building. London was developing rapidly and its financial heartland just happened to cosily embrace the fringes of the market before spreading back into the City. The elegant Victorian building quickly became swamped by modern office blocks and, although it was also a place where trading occurred, it was an anachronism amongst the shiny offices and pin-stripe suits. If it had just been the location, the market would have muddled on but there was a far more serious problem that threatened the survival of Billingsgate: traffic.

The increased traffic flowing around the ever-expanding City of London, plus the market traffic, combined to produce a daily bottleneck that put tremendous strain on the area. Lorries, pedestrians, taxis and cars vied for space where once there were just a few slow-moving horses and carts. Delivery lorries led to congestion that was bringing the whole area to a standstill every morning. A lorry park by the side of the market provided some much-needed space for the porters to load and unload the fish. But when Lower Thames Street was widened to try and deal with the traffic problem, porters had to run the gauntlet to push their trolleys back and forth across the road, as vehicles couldn't park close by any more. Billingsgate was left with only one option and that was to relocate.

It was no easy task to find a site in London that was big enough and accessible enough to become the home of the capital's great fish market. Eventually, after much searching and deliberating, an area on the then almost derelict Isle of Dogs was chosen. Lower Thames Street closed its doors for the final time on 16 January 1982 and Billingsgate was relocated to its current home. As yet, the prophecy of Old Billingsgate Market has yet to come to pass. It was said that once the cold store had been turned off, the frozen soil underneath would gradually melt and the entire building would collapse. In fact, the building still stands proudly and is now used for corporate functions.

Sourcing, Storing
& Preparing

Sourcing
Sustainable Seafood

Since the year 2000 the Billingsgate Seafood Training School has focused on promoting the health benefits of fish consumption as well as helping young and old alike to enjoy a wider variety of fish and shellfish. Increasing pressure on the wild resources of the sea has focused our work on promoting responsible sourcing of the lesser-known varieties that are predominantly available around European coasts. Sustainability and the responsible use of food from the sea is central in all aspects of our work, which includes working with young people, the public and the seafood industry.

Sourcing Responsibly

When considering the responsible sourcing of seafood we look at three main aspects – the stock size or amount of fish available, how the fish is caught and what happens to the product before it comes to Billingsgate. When fishing for particular species it is key that not too many are caught in any one year. By leaving a sufficient number of fish in the sea, a mature breeding stock will reproduce to give a healthy population (under good environmental conditions) for the next year. Increasingly, markets are looking towards fish farming and aquaculture to produce larger quantities of those fish that are in high demand. While this may offer some answers we need to consider issues such as what we are feeding these fish and how and where they are produced.

Fishing Responsibly

The way in which a wild fish is caught has a real impact on other species, particularly if they live in the same part of the sea as the target species. Fish without a viable market can easily be wasted as the fishermen will naturally want to fill their limited cargo hold with a product that is in demand. This certainly couples with our

work and our aim to raise consumer awareness of these less well-known fish and shellfish. We also promote fishing methods that target a particular type of fish, such as using hook and line, set nets, pots and traps. These methods cause less disruption to the marine habitat and target particular groups of fish. The selectivity of fishing methods is a measure of how many different shapes and sizes of fish are harvested by that method – the most sustainable fishing methods are highly selective and avoid a by-catch of unwanted marine animals.

Buying Responsibly

There are over 300 languages spoken in London, and people from many communities buy their fish from London's largest fish market, Billingsgate, where they know they can buy fish to suit a wide variety of cuisines. Indeed, the fabulous variety of fish and shellfish available makes Billingsgate a real magnet for those passionate about seafood. With such a selection you are really spoilt for choice. This choice is also widely available on our doorstep and we actively encourage School attendees to look for fish caught in local waters, thus trying to avoid processed products that carry excessive food miles.

If you are interested in learning more about seafood and sustainability visit www.goodcatch.org.uk, a 'one-stop-shop' sustainable seafood website created by the Marine Conservation Society (MCS), the Marine Stewardship Council (MSC), SeaWeb's Seafood Choices Alliance and Sustain.

**Adam Whittle, Deputy Director,
Billingsgate Seafood Training School**

Choosing & Buying Fish

Choosing which fish to buy at Billingsgate can be a fascinating experience. With typically over 150 species to choose from you are guaranteed to find something that takes your fancy, as well as some species you may not be familiar with. Follow the guidelines below to help you choose the best quality every time.

Whole Wet Fish

When buying whole fish there are some basic rules to follow in order to identify freshness:

- Look for fish with bright, vibrant colours and a glossy sheen.
- The eyes should be bright with a black convex pupil and clear cornea. Avoid any fish that have dull, sunken eyes.
- The gills should be bright red, not brown or grey.
- There should be clear slime on the fish and the skin should have an opalescent sheen. Avoid fish that look dull and any that have a sticky or congealing slime.
- Some fish will still be stiff with rigor mortis, indicating that the fish has been out of the water for 24 to 36 hours. If no longer in rigor mortis the fish should be firm to the touch. Avoid fish that are very soft to the touch or if the belly of the fish has split open.
- Fresh fish either has no smell or it will smell of the sea. Avoid any fish that have an unpleasant, sour smell, specifically of ammonia.
- The flesh should be firm and elastic and not 'pit' under gentle pressure.

Fish Fillets

With no eyes, gills and scales to aid in the identification of freshness, key things to focus on are:

- The fillets should have a good glossy sheen. Avoid those that are dull or discoloured.
- Fish fillets should be firm and the muscle bands will be tightly knitted together. Avoid fillets that show signs of the muscle beginning to separate.
- A fillet should smell of fresh sea air and have no bleached areas or discolouration. Avoid fillets that smell very strong or sour, specifically of ammonia.

Smoked Fish

Smoked fish should have a glossy sheen, firm flesh and a pleasant smoky aroma. Avoid fish that looks dull and smells unpleasant.

Shellfish

Shellfish are available in many different forms including raw, cooked, frozen, pre-packed and marinated. They can be classified as either crustacea or mollusc. Crustacean includes crab, lobster, prawns and langoustine while molluscs are sub-divided into 3 groups: bivalve, including oysters, mussels, clams, cockles and scallops; gastropod, including whelks and winkles; and cephalopod, being squid, cuttlefish and octopus.

Crab and lobster can be bought either live or pre-boiled. A boiled crab or lobster should have tight limbs and in the case of a lobster the tail should be attached to the body and be springy. Avoid any that have limp or loose limbs.

Prawns can be bought cooked, cooked and peeled, raw, frozen or marinated. To ensure maximum freshness:

- The shell of cooked prawns should be crisp and dry. Avoid those that are soft or wet to the touch.
- Prawns should smell pleasantly sweet and slightly of iodine. Avoid those that smell of ammonia.

Mussels, oysters and clams are sold either alive or cooked. When sold alive these shellfish come with a health mark that lists the common and Latin name of the species, dispatch centre, date of purchase and country of origin. This ensures that all these shellfish sold at Billingsgate market is premium quality. When alive the shells should be tightly closed or should close on tapping. Avoid those that are open or have damaged shells.

Scallops are sold in a variety of forms; live in the shell, as dry meat, soaked meat or frozen. There are two types of scallop; the larger king scallop and the smaller queen scallop (also know as 'queenies'). Unlike other bivalves scallops decompose slowly. Do not be overly concerned if the shells are not closed, have a look at the meat and as long as it is white and there are no 'off odours' they should be fine.

Whelks and periwinkles (winkles) are also available live and cooked on the market. They have a horny covering (operculum) that will close lightly over the opening of the univalve if tapped. They will also smell very strongly of ammonia if they are off.

Squid, cuttlefish and octopus should smell sweet and the flesh should be white. Avoid those that smell strongly and have a pink flesh.

Farmed Fish

Visitors to the market are often surprised by how much fish available is farmed (aquaculture). Recent figures show that around 45 per cent of all the fish consumed today is sourced this way. The range at Billingsgate is considerable and around 30 per cent of all fresh fish sales at the market are farmed salmon. Other farmed species available include large quantities of sea bass and sea bream, smaller quantities of farmed cod, halibut and turbot and very small quantities of sole. Fresh water species include tilapia, basa, trout, carp, pike and zander, and farmed shellfish available includes rope-grown mussels, clams, oysters and prawns.

We often talk to our guests about their views on farmed fish and the response is sometimes confusion as there are negative press reports regarding various environmental and social issues. Fish farming on a small 'survival' scale in the UK dates back several centuries when religious orders kept carp ponds to provide fish for the countless 'meatless' days dictated by the church. On a commercial scale fish farming is a rapidly expanding industry world-wide, but there have been some major teething troubles, particularly in developing countries. These include reports of damage to the environment including that caused by use of chemicals, reports of large quantities of fish kept in very close confinement, the quantity of wild fish catch needed to feed farmed fish and so forth.

Many issues have now been addressed or are being developed under close scrutiny. By proceeding carefully we should be able to look forward to an even larger selection of responsibly farmed fish in the future. As the world population grows many believe that fish farming is indeed the way forward as people understand the necessity to consume seafood as part of a healthy diet.

Frozen Fish

Frozen seafood is a continuous growth area for the market. It is easy to spot all the fresh fish but many don't appreciate that for every 15 kg (2 st 5 lb) of fresh fish sold there is around 10 kg (1 st 8 lb) of frozen. There is a large freezer at the back of the market that is stacked floor to ceiling with boxes of frozen product and set at around -26ºC (-14.8ºF) – a little time spent in the freezer makes a cold day on the market feel like the middle of summer! Many products are available ready-prepared and frozen. This includes many species of well-known seafood and is extremely good value. Choose fish that are well sealed in suitable packaging and show no signs of freezer burn (large dry white areas on the surface of the product).

Storing Fish

At the Market

The merchants at the market pack their wet fish products in ice and keep them refrigerated in large chillers, as close to 0ºC (32ºF) as possible. This keeps the product in peak condition. At the market most fish is sold as seen, so although some are sold prepared (gutted, filleted, skinned etc.), there are many that are in an unprepared state. See pages 27–39 for preparation techniques.

At Home

The best way to store most fish and to keep it in premium condition in the refrigerator is to keep it packed with ice or, if this isn't practical, with ice packs. Most domestic refrigerators are not cold enough to store fish for more than a day or two so always eat fresh fish as soon as possible after purchase. Ideally arrange the fish so that it is lying flat. The flakes of a fish are delicate and bending a fish in half can damage the flesh. For storing fish fillets we recommend that the fish is laid flat, cut in half or stacked flesh to flesh. Fish fillets need different handling to a whole fish and it is important to note that although they should be kept very cold and refrigerated, it is the skin only that should come into contact with ice and not the flesh. Smoked fish and live shellfish products need chilling, but not directly on ice. Place these products in a bowl or on a tray, cover with clingfilm and store towards the bottom of the refrigerator.

Tools
of the Trade

The tools of a fishmonger are fairly basic and do not need to cost a fortune. The block men and fishmongers that teach classes at the school bring in their own utensils as each have slightly different preferences as to the make of knife they choose to work with. They always guard their own equipment jealously and take pride in keeping each in the best condition. It often takes a little time to get used to using a new knife, so keep practising!

There are a handful of businesses at the market selling products to support the trade, including oils, potatoes and fish frying equipment along with work wear, fishmongers utensils and some catering supplies. When visiting the market it is possible to buy equipment from these suppliers, and some are also available from the school.

Filleting Knife

A sharp filleting knife is a key tool for fish preparation and is used to fillet and in some cases to skin a fish fillet. This knife has a flexible blade and this enables the blade to keep in close contact with either skin or bone. This knife should be kept sharp and not be used for other tasks.

Steaking Knife

A steaking knife is used for cutting larger fish including salmon and tuna loin into steaks. This knife can also be used to skin a large, wide fish fillet.

Pin Boners

These are not essential but can aid in the removal of the small pin bones located down the centre of a fish fillet. The pin bones can be removed with a pair of tweezers or cut out with a knife.

Fish Scaler

This tool removes the fish scales easily and safely and the scales are less likely to flick around the kitchen.

Nicker & Mallet

A nicker is used with a mallet to cut through very thick bone of larger fish including halibut and salmon. The tip of the nicker rests on the bone and a sharp tap from the mallet forces it through the bone without damaging the flesh in the immediate area.

Oyster Knife

An oyster knife is useful not only for shucking oysters but also for levering the shells of other molluscs including scallops.

Steel

A steel is essential to help keep the blade of a knife in good condition. Steels can be purchased from the school as part of the Training School wallet.

1. **Nicker**
2. **Pin Boners**
3. **Filleting knife**
4. **Steel**
5. **Steaking knife**
6. **Mallet**
7. **Oyster knife**
8. **Fish scaler**

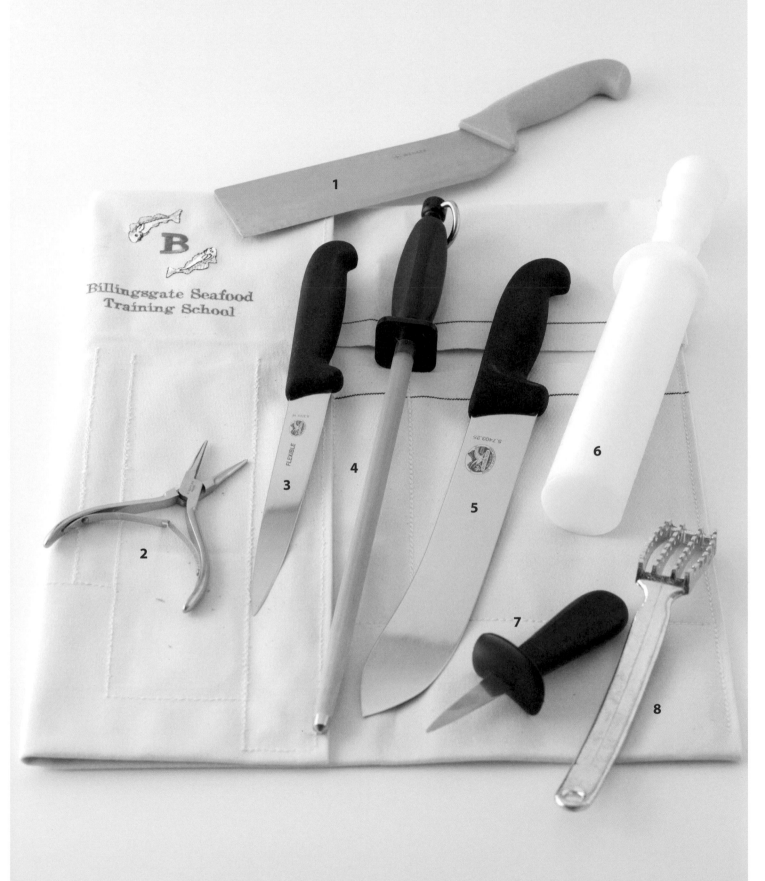

Fish Preparation
Techniques

Mick the Block Man

A number of first class chef and fishmonger trainers are employed by the Billingsgate Seafood Training School to deliver a wide variety of courses. One of these is block man Mick Mahoney who is loaned to the school by New England Seafood, a leading fish importer, wholesaler and processor of fresh fish. Here Mick shares his knowledge of fish preparation techniques.

Mick entered the fish trade by joining a London fishmonger as a trainee. He has since worked for Harrods, Selfridges, a kosher fishmonger in North London and for the last twelve years has been at New England Seafood. He has completed the Seafish Train the Trainer programme enabling him to deliver fishmonger training. He is just the sort of trainer that the school aims to work with; unassuming, patient, professional and an exceptional block man.

Preparing a Flat Fish to Cook Whole

1 Hold the fish by the tail and remove the fins using a pair of scissors, cutting from the tail towards the head.

2 Turn the fish over for ease and remove the remaining fins on the other side in the same way.

3 Cut the tail off using scissors.

4 Hold the fish by the head with your thumb on top and fingers in the gill flap. Cut around the head with a knife to mark through to the bone to prevent waste.

5 Cut through the bone to remove the head.

6 Using the tip of the knife and working away from you, remove the blood line. This is found near the head of the fish.

Filleting a Flat Fish (cross cut fillet)

1 Remove the head. Place the fish on a board with the dark side facing up. Insert the tip of the knife into the fillet just above the bone, keeping the back of the knife close to the back bone.

2 Keeping the back of the knife close to the back bone, push the knife forward keeping it above the skeleton. With a slow sawing action move the blade to the right, along the top of the bone and release the fillet at the fin.

3 Release the fillet at the tail end. Pull back the fillet to reveal the back bone with a long stroking action, ensuring that the fillet is released fully to the back bone. Hold the edge of the released fillet to reveal the back bone. Take the tip of the knife over the back bone and stroke along the second fillet to release.

4 In one long stroking action, and keeping the knife close to the bone, lift the fillet from the bone.

5 Continue stroking the knife along the bone to release the fillet at the fins.

Filleting a Flat Fish
(chefs' technique – quarter cross fillet)

1 Using the whole length of the knife cut through the skin and flesh to the back bone along the lateral (middle) of the fillet.

2 Right handers should work to the left fillet first, and vice versa for left handers. Run the tip of the knife along the back bone to release the first part of the fillet.

3 Turn the knife away from you and, using a long stroking action, work the knife from left to right, releasing the fillet at the fins.

4 Continue cutting to release the fillet. Turn the fish around so that the tail is pointing towards you and remove the second fillet in the same way.

Skinning a Dover Sole

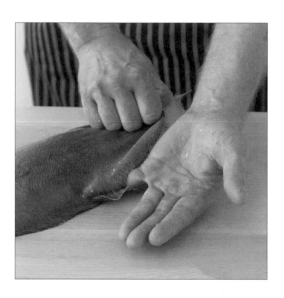

1 Hold the tip of the tail with your fingers. Mark through the skin to the bone without cutting all the way through. Starting with the tip of the knife pointing towards the head run the knife up and down the bone until the tip catches underneath the skin.

2 Insert a thumb or little finger under the skin and, running along the edge of the fillet close to the fins, release on one side of the skin.

3 Release the skin on the second side along the fillet close to the fins.

4 Hold the fish flat on the board with one hand (or use a cloth if it is slippery). Slowly pull the skin away from the body, taking care that the flesh doesn't rip.

Skinning a Gurnard

1 Hold the fish firmly by the tail. Using the heel of the knife and, starting at the tail end, cut under the dorsal fin using a short sharp cutting action. Tilt the knife towards the head to keep the knife close to the bone and avoid losing any flesh.

2 Remove the dorsal fin close to the head with scissors. Insert the scissors into the back of the head and cut through the back bone.

3 Using a cloth to protect your hands (as there are several very sharp fins) bend the head towards the belly and insert your index finger into the back of the fillet and lever apart.

4 Keeping the head close to the body and holding the top of the body with one hand, strip the head and skin away from the fish towards the tail end.

Steaking a Halibut

1 Using a nicker and mallet (see page 24), remove the tail of the fish.

2 Cut the head off then, using a steaking knife (see page 24), mark the fillets into even steaks of approximately 3 cm (1¼ in) wide.

3 Using the nicker and mallet, put the tip of the nicker on the bone and, in one sharp movement, hit with the mallet. This prevents the flesh from being damaged.

4 Trim the steaks and fillet the tail end of the fish (the part that is too narrow to cut into steaks).

5 Using the nicker and mallet cut each steak in half through the back bone.

Preparing a Round Fish to Cook Whole

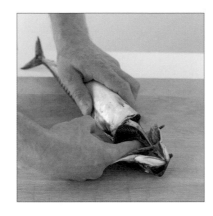

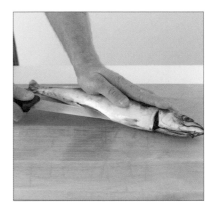

1 Lift the gill flap with a finger and carefully release the gills with the tip of the knife.

2 Insert your index finger under gills and pull away.

3 Working from tail to head, hold the fish securely by resting your free hand on the back of the fish. Insert the knife at the vent end of the fish, and with one long stroke cut along the belly to the head. Keep the knife parallel to the fish to avoid cutting into the fillets.

4 Remove the guts then, using the back of the knife, release the blood line and scrape away (this tastes bitter and must be removed before cooking).

5 To score the fish make small cuts through the skin into the fillet along the length of the fish.

Skinning a Monkfish

1 Working from head to tail, grasp the loose folds of skin.

2 Pull the skin away from the fish towards the tail (it releases easily).

3 To remove further membrane lie the fillet membrane-side down on the board. Starting at the tail end of the fillet and keeping the knife close to the membrane and skin, use a sawing action working towards the head.

Filleting a Monkfish Tail

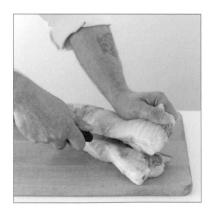

1 Starting at the thickest part of the fillet make a cut along the central bone.

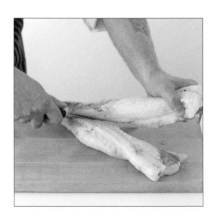

2 Using a long stroking action run the knife along the length of the bone to release one fillet.

3 Turn the fish over so that the bone is on the board and repeat the same process to remove the second fillet.

Skinning a Fish Fillet

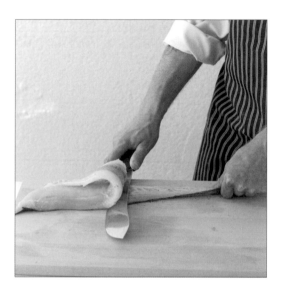

1 Choose a knife that is wide enough to work either side of the fillet. Starting at the thinnest part of the fillet (which is as the tail) and keeping the knife close to the skin, saw towards the head.

2 Keeping the knife at a 30 degree angle, pull the skin towards you as you push and cut away with the knife.

3 To pin bone the fish fillet, lay the fillet towards you and feel for the pin bones – they are situated at the thickest part of the fillet only, never at the tail end. Grasp the top of the pin bone with the pinboner and pull the bone away in the direction in which they grow. This prevents the fish from tearing.

Filleting a Salmon or Large Flat Fish

1 Make a cut into the back of the head with a knife.

2 Keeping the knife flat and working above the dorsal fin, run the knife along the back of the fish to open up the skin to reveal the flesh.

3 Once the tail end is released use long strokes to release the fillet.

4 Working from the tail towards the head continue releasing the fillet.

5 Using the tip of the knife, stroke over the top of the rib bones to lift the fillet away completely.

Steaking a Salmon

1 Fillet the loin.

2 Remove the head of the fish. Cut the top part of the fish above the dorsal fin and reserve to fillet as a loin. Mark the mid section of the fish into even steaks using a steaking knife.

3 The sectioned fish is now ready for cooking.

Preparing a Scaly Fish

2 Scale the fish with a scaler by holding onto the tail of and removing the scales, working from tail to head. This can be done with the fish lowered into a basin of cold water to prevent the scales from scattering around the kitchen.

1 Trim all the fins from the fish using a pair of scissors, always cut from tail to head for best results.

Filleting a Small Round Fish

1 Cut into the back of the head with a filleting knife.

2 Place the tip of the nicker (see page 24) onto the back bone and give one or two sharp taps with the mallet to cut through the bone.

3 Support the belly of the fish with your free hand. Keeping the knife flat and above the dorsal fin cut through the skin and, using a long stroking action, run the knife on top of the skeleton from head to tail to release the fillet.

4 Break the tail to give a point of exit on the underside of the fillet. Insert the knife through the back of the fish to the anal vent and cut along the bone to the tail until released.

5 Turn the knife away from you and make a cut towards the head end to release the back bone.

6 Hold the released part of the fillet in your free hand and, using the tip of the knife, stroke over the top of the rib bones to release the fillet.

Preparing a Squid

1 Pull the tentacles away from the main body.

2 Remove the beak from the centre of the tentacles.

3 Remove the quill-like cartilage from the middle of the squid.

4 Insert a thumb under the wings or fins.

5 Pull the fins away.

6 Pull away the membrane from the body of the squid.

7 To open the squid out flat, insert the knife into the inside and cut along the indentation left by the quill.

8 There are various ways of preparing the tubes – either cutting into rings, leaving whole or opening out into a sheet to score with a knife (as pictured).

9 The squid is now prepared and ready for cooking.

Cod, Haddock, Pollack, Coley & related species

What's on Offer

Of the many species of white fish on offer at the market, by far the best known is the cod family. Cod, the head of this large family of white, flaky-textured round fish, is related to haddock, coley, whiting, ling, pollack and hake. These species of fish are caught in the North Atlantic and surrounding waters.

Cod and haddock are popular choices with fish fryers who buy from the market. But coley and pollack particularly are seeing an increase of interest due to the positive reports regarding sustainability. Whiting is also a choice to consider. Fresh ling is rarely available. Hake is a white textured fish and is the most popular choice of the Spanish consumer. Supplies of hake are also imported from South Africa and South America.

Most of these fish are available in fillets, whole and gutted, head on or head off and frozen. Some of these fish are sold salted and others hot and cold smoked, so there is plenty to choose from. These fish are recognized by their distinctive markings and skin colour, but as with all fish on the market, it will be labelled with both its common and Latin name, making it impossible to mistake. The flesh of these fish is low in fat but not flavour. The flake of the fish means that they can break easily, but suit methods of cooking from simple baking or steaming to deep fat-frying.

Coley and pollack are both species that are used often in recipes at the school as our guests are interested in trying alternative white fish. Whole fish and fillets of both these species are used for teaching skinning techniques and pin-boning.

Cod and Haddock

Cod and haddock are well known for their white textured flesh and sweet flavour. Cod has a white lateral line on a marbled green skin, often with yellow specks. Haddock is the most easily recognized with a black lateral line and black mark on the shoulder of the fish, near the head, often referred to as St Peters mark.

Coley

Coley, often known as saithe or coalfish due to its black skin along the back of the fish, fading to silver on the belly, is densely scaly and has an obvious white lateral line. Up until fairly recently it was regarded as 'cat food', which is a real pity. It is an affordable fish and at the school we add it to our soups, casseroles and curries as it takes robust flavours well. It is also a favourite for use deep-fried in a beer (see page 45) or tempura batter (see page 186).

Pollack

Pollack is an excellent alternative to cod for those interested in trying something different. It has a deep olive green skin fading to silver on the belly with a thin silver lateral line that is slightly puckered, giving the appearance that it has been stitched. The fish has lovely flakes that retain moisture when cooked. It roasts well and has a sweet flavour.

Whiting

Whiting is sold whole and sometimes as fillets at the market. It has a silvery lateral line and pale, coppery coloured skin with large vibrant eyes. The flesh is incredibly delicate and low in fat. It is best enjoyed as fresh as possible as it softens and loses condition easily.

CLOCKWISE FROM TOP RIGHT: Coley (saithe) fillet, haddock fillet, pollack fillet, cod fillet, whole whiting.

White Fish

in Beer Batter

Serves 4

1 kg (2¼ lb) coley or tilapia fillet,
   unskinned
450 g (1 lb) Maris Piper potatoes,
   cut into chunky chips and soaked
   in cold water
4 tablespoons plain flour seasoned
   with salt and pepper
salt and freshly ground black
   pepper

FOR THE BATTER
100 g (4 oz) self-raising flour
½ teaspoon turmeric
½ teaspoon baking powder
½ teaspoon sea salt
250–300 ml (8–10 fl oz) pale ale

Skin on or off depends on personal taste, but many fish and chip shops choose to leave it on, which makes it easier to identify the fish. Although at the school we use a local brew, Greenwich Mean Time Pale Ale, in the batter, sparkling water is a good alternative to the beer if you prefer not to use alcohol.

Prepare the fish. Remove the pin bones but don't skin the fillets, then cut into equal sized portions.

In a bowl mix together the ingredients for the batter, adding just enough beer (or water) to make a smooth batter with the consistency of single cream.

Heat a deep-fat fryer to 160°C (325°F). Drain the chips on absorbent kitchen paper until thoroughly dry, then fry for 3–4 minutes to blanch. Lift directly on to a wire rack and pat dry with absorbent kitchen paper.

Increase the heat of the fryer to 170°C (340°F). Roll the fish in the seasoned flour and, using tongs, dip each piece in the batter. Holding the fish with tongs, carefully swish each piece back and forth in the hot oil for 10–15 seconds to allow the batter to set. Then release into the fryer completely. If you drop the fish into the oil straight away it will sink to the bottom and stick to the wire rack, and when you attempt to move it the batter coating will tear.

Cook the fish for 5–7 minutes or until the batter is golden-brown. Lift out on to a piece of absorbent kitchen paper. Pat dry and sprinkle lightly with salt. Keep warm on a wire rack in the oven.

Heat the oil to 180°C (350°F) and return the chips to the fryer for the second and final frying. When they are lightly browned lift on to a wire rack, season with salt and pepper, drain and serve along with the fried fish.

Try this with smoked haddock (a suggestion from Steve Pini, Executive Chef at Fishmongers' Hall) or pollack.

Goan Style
Seafood Curry   Serves 4

a selection of prepared fish, such as
  675g (1½ lb) white fish fillet (coley,
  hake or whiting), 350 g (12 oz)
  squid (tentacles removed) and
  12 tiger prawns (peeled and
  deveined)
50 g (2 oz) butter
2 onions, finely chopped
1 green chilli, seeded and finely
  chopped
3 cloves garlic, crushed
1 teaspoon fresh root ginger, peeled
  and grated
1 teaspoon chilli powder
½ teaspoon ground turmeric
1 teaspoon ground coriander
1 teaspoon ground cumin
6 tomatoes, skinned, seeded and
  chopped
1 tablespoon tomato purée
1 tablespoon tamarind pulp
410 g (14½ oz) can coconut milk
juice of ½ lime
salt and freshly ground black
  pepper
handful of coriander leaves,
  to garnish

TO SERVE
basmati rice, cooked according to
  the instructions on the packet

For our full-time courses we like to cover the preparation of a wide range of fish and seafood and as many cooking methods as possible. This curry has become a firm favourite at the school. Not only does it utilize a range of species, but it is also a dish that can easily be doubled or tripled, so it's great if you're feeding a crowd. It's also popular with the porters at the market and is often requested when we do our 'porters' breakfasts'.

If necessary, remove the pin bones from the fish fillets, cut into 5 cm (2 in) pieces and set aside. Open the squid out flat and cut into strips. Chill with the fish fillets and prawns until needed.

Melt the butter in a large saucepan, add the onions and cook over a gentle heat for 30 minutes or until soft and golden-brown. Stir in the chilli, garlic and ginger and continue to cook for 3 minutes. Add the spices and cook for a further 2 minutes.

Add the tomatoes, tomato purée and tamarind pulp and cook for a further couple of minutes. Add the coconut milk to the saucepan, bring to the boil and simmer for 5 minutes. Add the white fish pieces and prawns and cook over a gentle heat for 3 minutes, then add the squid and cook until the fish is opaque. Lift the fish from the cooking liquid and keep warm.

Reduce the sauce if necessary by boiling rapidly. Add the lime juice and season to taste with salt and pepper. Stir the coriander leaves into the curry and replace the fish. Serve with basmati rice.

Bacon-wrapped
White Fish

Serves 4

8 rashers of streaky bacon
50 g (2 oz) sun-blushed tomatoes,
  roughly chopped
1 tablespoon toasted pine nuts
1 tablespoon chopped fresh herbs,
  including basil and parsley
4 fillets of white fish, such as pollack,
  each about 170 g (6 oz)
freshly ground black pepper
rocket leaves or sprigs of watercress

Try this with gurnard,
tilapia or pollack

Most of the recipes we use at the school are designed for ease and simplicity, and this recipe is something we often cook. Try it with pancetta or thinly sliced chorizo instead of streaky bacon.

Preheat the oven to 200°C/400°F/gas mark 6.

Place 2 rashers of bacon on a board and stretch flat with the back of a knife. Sprinkle with a quarter of the tomatoes, pine nuts and herbs. Arrange a fillet on top and wrap the bacon around to form a small parcel. Transfer to a baking sheet and season lightly with pepper. Wrap the remaining fillets in the same way.

Cook the fish for 12–16 minutes or until it is opaque and feels firm to the touch and the bacon is browned. Serve with a garnish of rocket or watercress.

"I eat haddock from the chippie with mushy peas and curry sauce. I'm from Sheffield so I get called 'mushy' cos we love our mushy peas up north!"

Mike ("Mushy"), James Nash & sons

Whiting Armandine

Serves 4

4 **whiting fillets, skinned and**
   pin-boned
3 **tablespoons plain flour seasoned**
   with salt and pepper
2 **rashers of streaky bacon, finely**
   diced
1 **tablespoon olive oil**
50 g (2 oz) butter
75 g (3 oz) flaked almonds
2 **tablespoons chopped parsley**
salt and freshly ground black
   pepper
squeeze of lemon juice (to taste)

Try this with trout or
grey mullet fillets

Fresh whiting is a really sensational fish and we get the pick of the best from the market. Fish of such high quality requires only light cooking and delicate flavours, and this is an excellent combination.

Roll the whiting fillets in the seasoned flour and arrange in a single layer on a plate. Fry the bacon in a nonstick frying pan until it is crisp and the fat has been released. Lift the bacon on to a plate.

Add the oil and a small piece of butter to the pan and heat until the butter has stopped sizzling and is beginning to brown. Add the whiting fillets, two at a time, and pan-fry for 2–3 minutes on each side or until the fish is just cooked. Transfer to a plate and keep warm. Wipe the frying pan with absorbent kitchen paper.

Return the pan to the heat and add the remaining butter. Allow to melt and begin to brown, add the almonds and stir constantly over a medium heat until they are nut brown. Add the parsley and replace the bacon, season lightly and at the last minute splash in some lemon juice. Quickly swirl the pan around to draw the ingredients together, then pour over the fish and serve immediately.

"A whiting at its best is absolutely superb. Fillet it and treat it with the respect you would give a Dover sole – lightly pan-fried it's just lovely."

Charlie Casey M.B.E., retired fishmonger and occasional trainer at the school

Crusted Pollack
with Parsley & Mustard

Serves 2

1 small pollack fillet, about 300 g (11 oz), skinned

FOR THE CRUST
1 tablespoon Dijon mustard
3 tablespoons finely chopped parsley
3 tablespoons melted butter
5 tablespoons fresh breadcrumbs
salt and freshly ground black pepper

TO SERVE
green salad
new potatoes

This recipe works well with most white fish, and at the school we not only use pollack but also red gurnard, coley, tilapia and mullet.

Preheat the oven to 200°C/400°F/gas mark 6. Remove any pin bones from the pollack and put on a baking sheet.

Make the crust. In a bowl mix together the mustard, parsley, butter and breadcrumbs and season lightly with salt and pepper. Spread over the skinned side of the pollack.

Bake in the oven for 12–15 minutes or until the pollack is cooked; it should be white and opaque and look flaky. Serve with a simple salad and new potatoes.

Try this with coley or hake

Billingsgate School
Fish Pie

Serves 6

450 g (1 lb) white fish fillets, such as coley, hake or pollack
900 ml (1½ pints) semi-skimmed milk
1 bay leaf
90 g (3½ oz) butter
1 leek, finely sliced
90 g (3½ oz) plain flour
¼ teaspoon cayenne pepper
¼ teaspoon freshly grated nutmeg
½ teaspoon dried English mustard
3 hard-boiled eggs, quartered
2 tablespoons chopped dill
2 tablespoons chopped parsley
salt and freshly ground black pepper

FOR THE MASHED POTATO TOPPING
1 k g (2¼ lb) King Edward potatoes, peeled
25 g (1 oz) butter
120–150 ml (4–5 fl oz) hot milk
salt and freshly ground black pepper
1–2 tablespoons grated Cheddar cheese

This great fish pie is something that we cook for guests who attend our lecture-based courses, and it's become a firm favourite.

Preheat the oven to 190°C/375°F/gas mark 5.

Put the fish in a large sauté pan, pour over the milk and add the bay leaf. Bring to the boil, reduce the heat and poach over a low heat for 4–5 minutes or until the fish is cooked. Strain the milk into a jug and set aside. Remove the skin and any pin bones from the fish. Discard the bay leaf.

Heat the butter in a saucepan and cook the leek for 4–5 minutes or until soft. Stir in the flour, cayenne pepper, nutmeg and mustard and cook for a further 1 minute. Carefully blend in the reserved milk, bring to the boil, stirring continuously, and allow to simmer for 2–3 minutes. Add the hard-boiled eggs, herbs and fish and season to taste with salt and pepper. Pour into a large ovenproof pie dish.

Meanwhile, prepare the topping. Cook the potatoes in boiling salted water until tender. Drain and return to the pan to dry for 1 minute over a very low heat. Mash thoroughly, blending in the butter and hot milk. Season to taste with salt and pepper and spoon over the fish. Fork up the top of the pie and sprinkle with the cheese.

Bake in the oven for 20–25 minutes or until the topping is golden-brown and the whole pie is piping hot and bubbling.

Try this with any mixture of white fish. Shellfish, including prawns, cooked mussels and clams (removed from the shell), are a great addition

Fishmongers' Company

Throughout much of the history of Billingsgate, behind the hustle and bustle of the market, The Worshipful Company of Fishmongers (or Fishmongers' Company) has played an active role. The Company is one of the Twelve Great Livery Companies of the City of London and has a history that stretches back over 700 years. Livery Companies were initially set up to help regulate and oversee their respective trades. Over the years, as trades and certain skills vanished or were rendered obsolete by modern technology, so the livery companies were no longer required on an everyday basis. However, the Fishmongers' Company remains an integral part of the modern fishing industry and is very much alive and well at Billingsgate. Many Livery Companies have impressive headquarters or halls, but the Fishmongers' can surely stake a claim to being the most striking. Perched on the north side of London Bridge, close to Old Billingsgate Market, the building is a fitting tribute to its trade.

Ready for Inspection

The Fishmongers' Company traditionally had some hefty responsibilities and a succession of charters in the thirteenth and fourteenth centuries granted them the authority to inspect any fish sold in the City of London. This was no easy task, as fish was sold in hundreds of shops, stalls and eateries, as well as the market, and health and safety probably wasn't top of every vendor's list of priorities in those days. Although, in theory, the Company still has the power to inspect and condemn fish anywhere in the City, nowadays they generally just deal with Billingsgate. Although the new Billingsgate Market isn't geographically in the City of London – it's in Tower Hamlets – an Act in 1979 ensured that the Fishmongers' Company could remain as custodians of quality control when the market moved to its new location. Today, there are three inspectors who work at the market, with someone on the premises at all times. Although they work there every day, the inspectors are completely autonomous of Billingsgate, which ensures they can perform their role with greater independence.

All in a Day's Work

The inspectors have a number of roles that relate to many areas of the market, from quality control to education, and they need to be a visible presence in order to maintain the trust and respect of both the merchants and the customers. Obviously, the main role they perform is to ensure that all the fish sold in the market is fresh and fit for human consumption. Fish is highly perishable and there are strict regulations in place.

There are a number of criteria the inspectors use when they check fish and these include making sure the eyes are clear, bright and fresh; checking that the gills move apart and have a good colour; making sure the flesh is nice and firm; and looking for any damage to the skin and scales. However, years of experience mean that an inspector can spot a substandard specimen at fifty paces and any dubious stock will be dealt with in a flash without drawing unnecessary attention to the merchant. There's generally little argument once the inspector has made their decision: mutual respect means that decisions are taken on the chin and there's usually no more than a quiet grumble when they pause and point at dubious stock. Merchants and inspectors know that with such a perishable commodity the condition of fish can change very rapidly and checks must be made frequently to maintain the reputation of the market and the health of the consumer. It's in everyone's interests for the market to sell the freshest seafood of the highest quality.

Red Mullet, Grey Mullet, Sea Bass & Bream

What's on Offer

There are many sea fish for sale on the market that have a white textured flesh with a heavy armoring of scales that need to be removed prior to cooking. These fish include red and grey mullet, sea bass, sea bream, snapper and barramundi, to mention a few.

Sea Bass

Sea bass, both farmed and wild, are readily available at the market and are considered to be premium fish due to its high demand by restaurants. Sold whole and often uncleaned or as fillets, farmed bass comes from the Mediterranean along with farmed gilt head bream. These are grown to a uniform size and appeal particularly to chefs as they produce excellent single serving sized fillets. Wild bass, on the other hand, can vary quite dramatically in size and potentially poses a different challenge to a chef. It comes from a variety of sources and reaches the market so quickly that it is often still in rigor mortis. These fish tend to be larger, the minimum legal catch size being (at the time of publication) 36 cm (14 in) whereas farmed fish is usually smaller than this. Although the flavour of the farmed fish is excellent, wild bass is a real treat and is quite affordable if buying from the market, but be prepared to buy a whole fish and to trim, scale and clean it yourself. The price, as with all wild fish, is never set and will fluctuate, although the value of the fish usually increases with size.

There is a very small fishery on the east coast for bass, which is certified by the MSC (Marine Stewardship Council) as sustainable, but 'line caught' wild bass from the South Coast or the Channel Islands is a very environmentally friendly alternative.

FROM LEFT TO RIGHT: red mullet, gilt head sea bream, grey mullet, sea bass.

Gilt Head Bream

This is extensively farmed in the Mediterranean and is in plentiful supply at the market. Although sea bass tends to be the more popular species in the UK, bream is widely considered to be the best flavoured of the two, certainly in the Mediterranean. Other varieties of wild bream are also often available including pink bream (also known as rose dorade), black bream and occasionally Ray's bream. Various warm water bream such as thread fin bream can also be found. These fish are extremely versatile and can be used in many different recipes and styles of cooking including en papillote, steaming, pan-frying, poaching, roasting whole or grilling.

Red Mullet

Red Mullet is often found at the market and comes from a variety of sources. People are sometimes surprised to learn that such excellent quality and responsibly caught fish comes up from the south coast of the UK and Ireland during the summer as red mullet is often associated with the Mediterranean. There is no size limit in the Mediterranean and therefore very small and immature fish are often seen for sale in the many small fish markets all along the coast of Southern Europe. Fish landed in the UK are larger, mature fish that have had the chance to breed and are a better choice in terms of sustainability of the stock.

Sold whole and usually ungutted this fish needs trimming, scaling and gutting at home. The liver of this fish is a delicacy and should be retained and enjoyed. Red mullet is used at the school to demonstrate various preparation techniques, including trimming the fish of extremely sharp bones, scaling and gutting.

Billingsgate Merchants'
Fish Soup

Serves 6

1 kg (2¼ lb) white fish fillets, including hake, red gurnard and grey mullet
250 g (9 oz) tiger prawns, peeled and deveined
4 tablespoons extra virgin olive oil
2 cloves garlic, crushed
1 red chilli, seeded and finely chopped
1 onion, finely chopped
1 large leek, white part only, finely sliced
½ bulb Florence fennel, finely sliced
1 teaspoon tomato purée
1 teaspoon fennel seeds
150 ml (5 fl oz) can chopped tomatoes
2 tablespoons chopped parsley
1 bay leaf
1 teaspoon thyme leaves
generous pinch of saffron
1–2 teaspoons grated orange zest
85 ml (3 fl oz) dry white wine
750 ml (1¼ pints) fish stock
450 g (1 lb) mussels or Venus clams, cleaned and debearded
a splash of Pernod
salt and freshly ground black pepper

TO SERVE
toasted baguette
1 serving of rouille

This is a favourite recipe at the school. You can use just about any fish or seafood to make the soup and we use many different species. We also always make stock with the trimmings, such as is required for this recipe.

Prepare the fish. Cut the fillets into 3–4 cm (1½ in) pieces and set aside. Peel, devein and butterfly the prawns. Keep chilled until required.

Heat the olive oil in a large saucepan, add the garlic, chilli, onion, leek and fennel and cook over a low heat for 4–5 minutes. Add the tomato purée and fennel seeds and continue to cook for another 2 minutes, then add the remaining ingredients. Bring to the boil, stirring occasionally, and simmer vigorously for 8–10 minutes, until the oil and liquid are emulsified.

Add the fish fillets, prawns and mussels or clams and cook over a low heat for 3–4 minutes or until nearly cooked and the mussels are beginning to open. Season to taste with salt and pepper and a splash of Pernod. Serve the soup with slices of toasted baguette and rouille.

Rouille

There are many different recipes for this hot pepper and garlic paste. It originates from the Mediterranean and is classically served with fish soups and stews, such as bouillabaisse, but it is delicious served with any fried fish and with salt cod.

3 cloves garlic, crushed
1 tablespoon harissa paste
3 red peppers, halved, seeded, grilled and peeled
6 tablespoons olive oil
4 tablespoons fresh white breadcrumbs
salt and freshly ground black pepper
2 tablespoons mayonnaise

Blend the garlic, harissa paste and red peppers in a liquidizer until smooth. With the motor still running, slowly pour the oil in to the purée. Add the breadcrumbs to bind the sauce. Season to taste with salt and pepper and stir in the mayonnaise.

Tapenade Crumbed
Fish with Warm Fennel Salad

4 white fish fillets, 170 g (6 oz) each
2 tablespoons green olive tapenade
8 tablespoons fresh breadcrumbs
2 tablespoons freshly grated
   Parmesan cheese
sprigs of basil, to garnish

FOR THE SALAD
2 tablespoons extra virgin olive oil
1 clove garlic, crushed
2 tablespoons chopped basil
grated zest and juice of 1 lime
1 bulb Florence fennel, sliced
150 g (5 oz) cherry tomatoes, halved
salt and freshly ground black
   pepper

Preheat the oven to 190°C/375°F/gas mark 5.

Skin the fish if necessary and arrange on a baking sheet. In a bowl mix together the tapenade, breadcrumbs and Parmesan, sprinkle the mixture over the fish and bake in the oven for 12–15 minutes or until the fish is just cooked.

Heat the oil in a saucepan, add the garlic and basil and infuse over a low heat for 2–3 minutes. Add the lime zest, fennel and cherry tomatoes and cook for 1 minute. Remove from the heat and add the lime juice and season to taste with salt and pepper.

Pile the warm fennel salad on to a large serving dish and arrange the crumbed fish fillets on top. Garnish with sprigs of basil and serve warm.

Try this with coley, pollack or tilapia

Sea Bass

& Fennel Tray Roast   Serves 4

2 small sea bass, filleted
2 bulbs Florence fennel, finely sliced
1 red onion, finely sliced
3 tablespoons extra virgin olive oil
salt and freshly ground black
    pepper
1 tablespoon oregano leaves
splash of Pernod
juice of ½ lemon and a few lemon
    wedges

Preheat the oven to 220°C/425°F/gas mark 7. Pin-bone the sea bass fillets, score the skin with a sharp knife and season.

Put the fennel and onion in a large roasting tin. Drizzle with olive oil and season with salt and pepper. Bake in the oven for 7 minutes.

Remove the vegetables from the oven and sprinkle with the oregano leaves. Arrange the fish on top. Splash with a little Pernod and lemon juice and tuck lemon wedges around the edge. Return to the oven for a further 7–10 minutes or until the fish is cooked; the flesh will be opaque and the skin will peel away easily. Serve straight from the roasting tin.

Try this with sea bream, red mullet or trout

"I like a nice sea bass steamed & served up with tinned potatoes. No veg though, just the tinned potatoes." **Deano, James Nash & Sons**

Steamed
Sea Bass Parcels

with Salsa Rosso   Serves 2

4 sea bass fillets
splash of extra virgin olive oil
splash of white wine
salt and freshly ground black
  pepper

TO SERVE
2 tablespoons Salsa Rosso
handful of rocket leaves
lemon wedges

Try this with sea bream,
salmon or pollack

Preheat the oven to 220°C/425°F/gas mark 7.

Pin-bone the fish fillets (see page 35). Cut 2 heart shapes from pieces of good-quality greaseproof paper about 60 cm (24 in) long and fold them in half to crease the centre line. Put half the fish fillets on one side of the heart shape, drizzle with half of the olive oil and white wine. Season lightly. Repeat with the remaining ingredients to make a second parcel. Wrap the fish securely, but not too closely, in the greaseproof paper so that the steam can circulate. Roast in the oven for 12–15 minutes or until cooked; the flesh will be firm and opaque.

Open the parcels, spoon over the Salsa Rosso (red sauce) and a small handful of rocket, garnish with lemon wedges and serve.

Salsa Rosso

2 tablespoons olive oil
1 clove garlic, peeled and finely chopped
1 fresh red chilli, seeded and finely chopped
1 tablespoon chopped marjoram leaves
200 g (7 oz) can plum tomatoes, drained
2 red peppers, grilled, skinned, seeded and finely chopped
sea salt and freshly ground black pepper
2 small dried chillies, crumbled (optional)

Heat the olive oil in a saucepan and gently fry the garlic until it starts to colour. Add the chilli, marjoram and tomatoes and cook for 10 minutes or until the tomatoes are reduced. Add the peppers and cook for a further 10 minutes. Season with sea salt and pepper, adding dried chilli as an extra seasoning if liked

Steamed
Sea Bass
with Lettuce   Serves 2

4 small sea bass fillets, unskinned
large cos (romaine) lettuce leaves
2 spring onions, very finely sliced
2 tablespoons chopped sun-
    blushed tomatoes
salt and freshly ground black
    pepper

TO SERVE
olive oil (optional)
lemon wedges

Take a saucepan that is large enough to fit a bamboo steamer on top and bring water to the boil. Pin-bone the fish fillets if necessary (see page 35).

Blanch 4 large lettuce leaves in the boiling water for 15–20 seconds, rinse in cold water and pat dry on absorbent kitchen paper. Cut out the central core of the lettuce leaves so that they will lie flat.

Arrange a fish fillet on each lettuce leaf, sprinkle with spring onions and tomatoes and season lightly. Wrap the leaf around the fish and arrange them on a steamer so the fish are flat. Cover and cook for 5–7 minutes or until the fish has lost its translucency.

Transfer to 2 serving plates, drizzle with a little olive oil and serve with lemon wedges.

Simply Roasted
Bass & Bream   Serves 4
with Herbs & Citrus

4 small sea bass fillets, unskinned
4 small sea bream fillets, unskinned
    and pin-boned
coarsely ground sea salt and freshly
    ground black pepper
3 tablespoons extra virgin olive oil
2 cloves garlic, unpeeled
grated zest and juice of 1 lemon or
    lime
sprigs of rosemary or dill

Pin-bone the fish fillets (see page 35). Using a sharp knife, lightly score the skin of the fish, taking care not to cut too deeply into the flesh. Put the fish in a roasting tin, skin side up, rub the skin with sea salt, pepper and drizzle with oil. Arrange the garlic cloves around the sides. Sprinkle with the citrus juice and zest and the chosen herb. Leave to marinate for 10 minutes.

Preheat the oven to 200°C/400°F/gas mark 6. Roast the fish for 12–14 minutes or until the flesh is opaque and firm to the touch.

Serve each diner with one bass and one bream fillet and drizzle over the cooking juices.

Sea Bream & Tiger Prawn en Papillotte

Serves 2

2 small sea bream fillets
4 tablespoons extra virgin olive oil
1 clove garlic, sliced
small handful of herbs, including
  basil, flat leaf parsley and
  tarragon, leaves only, shredded
175 g (6 oz) raw tiger prawns, peeled
2 tablespoons white wine
salt and freshly ground black
  pepper

Try this with sea bass

Preheat the oven to 220°C/425°F/gas mark 7. Preheat a baking sheet in the oven. Cut out 2 heart shapes from pieces of good-quality greaseproof paper about 60 cm (24 in) long and fold them in half to crease the centre line. Pin-bone the fish fillets (see page 35).

Heat the oil in a small pan, add the garlic and herbs and cook over a low heat for 2–3 minutes or until the oil is well infused. Remove from the heat and allow to cool.

Arrange half the fish on one side of a greaseproof paper heart. Arrange half the prawns around the edge. Spoon half the infused oil and wine over the top and season lightly. Repeat with the remaining ingredients in the other greaseproof paper heart.

Wrap the fish securely, but not too closely, in the greaseproof paper, so that the steam can circulate but not escape. Place on the heated baking sheet and cook in the oven for 12–15 minutes or until cooked; the flesh will be firm and opaque. Serve the fish directly from the paper and allow your guests to open at the table.

The City of London

There are four ancient markets that are run by the City of London and have been for many hundreds of years. Although historically interesting in itself, it is made all the more intriguing by the fact that two of them are no longer located in the City. Both Billingsgate and Spitalfields have moved to new premises but they continue to come under the City jurisdiction with The City of London acting as both owner and landlord. It's an unusual scenario to have little pockets of a borough that are effectively controlled by the original heartland of ancient London. It is a testament to London's incredible history, growth and adaptability that such arrangements are not just possible but extremely effective. In order to ensure a consistent administration system The City of London appoints a Superintendent for each market. They are effectively the on-site manager, in charge of the daily running of the market and they head a team of staff that deals with everything from finance to health and safety matters.

Smooth Operation

A market is a community, a business, a centre of commerce and a workplace. In order to create an effective environment in which to shop and work, there's an awful lot of action behind the scenes. While the merchants ply their wares in the market hall, the corridors and offices upstairs buzz with the sound of phones ringing and keys being tapped, as the administration side of Billingsgate ensures everything runs smoothly. Although the office hours are slightly more sociable than those of the merchants and porters, everyone is working with the same aim: to keep the market running successfully and to increase people's awareness of it.

The Market Superintendent is at the top of the administration food chain and is in charge of 33 staff at Billingsgate. This is made up of a range of administration support and Market Constables and they come under the City of London payroll. However, there's another extremely important band of workers whose crucial role ensures that the market is cleaned to exacting standards every day. With such perishable and, let's be honest, odoriferous stock, cleanliness

is a big issue for Billingsgate and the cleaning team are nothing short of miracle workers. Once trading ceases, there's a sea of water, a mountain of boxes and a veritable smorgasbord of fishy odds and ends adorning the market hall. However, by 3pm the place is spotless, the floors have been washed and even the car park is pristine. Although sea gulls still loiter about looking for scraps, they generally leave with empty bellies if they arrive mid-afternoon.

Security

There are 14 Market Constables at Billingsgate and there is security cover 24 hours a day, seven days a week. Busier times require more feet on the beat and the Superintendent tries to ensure as many Constables are on duty as possible between the hours of 4am and 9am, Tuesday to Saturday. The Constables are not Police Officers but are employed directly by the City of London to carry out security duties in and around the market. With people, cars, lorries and trolleys creating a market rush hour every morning, many of their duties involve traffic and crowd control. The main aim of the Market Constables is to ensure that both merchants and customers can conduct their business safely and efficiently. Their training enables them to effectively diffuse any potentially difficult situations and their uniform makes them a reassuring presence throughout the market.

Going Green

One of the big costs for the market is waste disposal and it's hardly surprising considering the sheer amount of boxes and other packaging that arrives on site every day. It's no mean feat for a market to earn a reputation for being a recycling innovator but Billingsgate is rightly proud of its green credentials. In November 2007 the market was the first site in the country to install a 'Clean Heat Packer', which basically melts down polystyrene boxes into blocks. As polystyrene accounts for an incredible 80 per cent of waste at Billingsgate this has resulted in a huge reduction in landfill, as well as cutting the disposal bill in half.

Gurnard, John Dory & Monkfish

What's on Offer

There is a good selection of species on the market that require particular techniques for preparation. The fish that we particularly use at the school include John Dory, gurnard and monkfish.

Gurnard

Gurnard is an interesting looking fish and people often mistake them for other red-coloured species including red mullet. There are three types of gurnard available – red, grey and yellow – red being the most predominant species at the market. It has gained popularity, especially with us over the last few years as it does have a great flavour. There is quite a low yield to body weight, so for our courses we aim to choose the largest specimens we can. In terms of sustainability the Marine Conservation Society includes red gurnard on their 'fish to eat' list.

Although there is quite a lot of weight lost in the bones, skin and head of a gurnard, these trimmings do make superb stock. As with any fish it is important to remove traces of blood and guts, but once the gills are removed the head, fins and skin give excellent flavour. This fish can be roasted, grilled (we use it for steaming or en papillote), but as it is low in fat and delicate it usually benefits from a light brushing of oil or a jacket of bacon or pancetta to keep it moist during cooking. It has also been presented recently in a handful of fish and chip shops – battered and deep-fried. The batter keeps the fish moist and is worth trying. At the school we teach a preparation technique that shows removing fins, head

and skin to reveal a small tail of gurnard (see page 31). This fish is very best cooked on the bone for added flavour.

Monkfish

Monkfish, also known as angler fish, is another popular and premium fish found on the market. The story of its rise to stardom is popular press, but up until the 1970's it was not particularly well-known and was often cut and sold as scampi, as the texture of the flesh is dense and meaty. It was Fanny Craddock, the 1960's TV cook, who drew attention to it as a fish of great flavour – once discovered, never forgotten – and it is now popular. The fish that arrives at the market comes from various sources but most often are gutted and headless. The heads are removed at source and the cheeks removed and sold separately. The head is heavy and would add extra weight to a box of fish to be transported.

This fish is a good choice for those who do not like bones as once the back bone is removed there are no others. It suits many methods of cooking and is particularly good for stir-frying as the texture is such that it doesn't break up. It has a unique flavour all of its own and takes robust flavours, particularly spices, very well.

At the school we only occasionally work with monkfish tails. We teach how to skin and trim away the various layers of membrane that have to be removed as they shrink and become tough on cooking. We also demonstrate the ease of filleting this fish for use at home.

FROM LEFT TO RIGHT: John Dory and red gurnard.

John Dory

John Dory is called Saint Pierre in France due to the St Peters mark on the shoulder of the fish. It is an interesting looking fish, being laterally compressed, which makes them difficult to see head on and great for sneaking up on its prey. It has a large retractable jaw that virtually vacuums its prey as the jaw extends easily. It is very bony and has sharp fins making it a challenge to prepare, but it is one of the very best flavoured fish in the sea! It is not available in large quantities at the market and its quality makes it highly sought after, which can be reflected in the price. Like gurnard the flesh yield to bone is quite low, as much as 60 per cent is waste, although the trimmings and head make excellent stock.

Only available whole and gutted, it can be trimmed of all the sharp barbs, rolled in flour and pan-fried. Alternatively the fish can be filleted (using the Cross Cut Method – see page 28). The skin is soft and can be left on to help hold the fillets together for pan-frying – pull the skin away and each side of the fish will naturally break into three small sections.

At the school we use John Dory occasionally to show trimming of extremely sharp fins and barbs around the fillet of the fish. We sometimes prepare this to pan-fry whole or use a filleting technique particular for this species.

Grilled Monkfish
& Bay Leaf Skewers

Serves 2

**1 small monkfish tail, about 450 g
    (1 lb)**
5 tablespoons white wine vinegar
10 bay leaves
2 tablespoons extra virgin olive oil
**salt and freshly ground black
    pepper**

TO SERVE
handful of salad leaves

Prepare the monkfish tail (see page 34). Cut the fish into pieces about 3 cm (1¼ in) thick, lay them in a single layer in a shallow dish and sprinkle with white wine vinegar. Cover and refrigerate for a couple of hours.

Preheat the grill to its highest setting. Thread the marinated fish on to wooden skewers, adding a bay leaf every so often. Drizzle the skewers with olive oil and season generously with pepper and a little salt.

Arrange the skewers on a grill rack and cook on a low shelf under the grill for 4–5 minutes or until the fish is cooked; it will be translucent and firm. Serve on a bed of salad leaves.

Try this with raw tiger prawns

John Dory

Serves 4

with Lemon Thyme & Wild Mushrooms

8 John Dory fillets, unskinned

3 tablespoons plain flour seasoned
   with salt, pepper and a pinch of
   freshly grated nutmeg

1 tablespoon lemon thyme leaves

50 g (2 oz) butter

1 tablespoon olive oil

1 clove garlic, crushed

100 g (4 oz) wild mushrooms, such as
   chanterelles and oyster
   mushrooms, thickly sliced

2 tablespoons white wine

lemon juice, to taste

8 tablespoons double cream

salt and freshly ground black
   pepper

Roll the fish fillets in the seasoned flour.

Put the lemon thyme leaves, half the butter and all the olive oil in a nonstick frying pan and heat until the butter stops sizzling and just begins to brown. Add the fish, skin side down, and pan-fry for 2–3 minutes on each side or until cooked; the fish will be opaque and firm to the touch. Transfer the fish to a serving plate and keep warm.

In a separate pan melt the remaining butter until foaming. Add the garlic and mushrooms and cook over a low heat until just cooked through. Add the wine, bring to the boil and simmer until completely reduced. Add a splash of lemon juice and stir in the cream, bring to the boil and season to taste. Pour over the fish to serve.

Try this with any flat fish fillet

Pan-fried Monkfish

with Avocado, Lime & Coriander Dressing

Serves 2

1 small monkfish tail, about 450 g
  (1 lb), filleted, skinned and
  trimmed (see page 34)
1 teaspoon ground coriander
2 tablespoons extra virgin olive oil
1 whole clove garlic
½ red chilli

FOR THE DRESSING
grated zest and juice of 1 lime
2 teaspoons fish sauce
1 tablespoon palm sugar
salt and freshly ground black
  pepper
1 ripe avocado, stoned, skinned
  and diced
3 spring onions, finely sliced
large handful of coriander,
  roughly chopped

Cut the fish into 8 medallions and season with ground coriander. Heat the oil in a large frying pan, add the garlic and chilli and fry for 1–2 minutes over a low heat just to infuse the oil. Remove and discard the garlic and chilli. Increase the heat, add the fish and fry for 2–3 minutes on each side or until the fish is firm to the touch and opaque in appearance. Set aside.

In a large bowl combine the lime zest and juice, fish sauce and palm sugar. Season lightly with salt and pepper and toss in the avocado, spring onions, coriander and warm monkfish medallions, check the seasoning and pile on a large serving platter.

Try this with brill, turbot or add prawns

"I was introduced to monkfish 50 years ago. We used to buy 'catflaps' (boxes of fish trimmings including cod and belly flaps). Monkfish tails ended up in there as no-one wanted them. I though they were great."

Charlie Casey M.B.E., retired fishmonger and occasional trainer at the school

Monkfish Tagine

with Lemon & Olives

Serves 4

**675 g (1½ lb) monkfish fillet, skinned
and thickly sliced**
1 teaspoon ground cumin
2 tablespoons extra virgin olive oil
1 large onion, finely chopped
2 cloves garlic, crushed
large pinch of saffron
½ teaspoon ground cinnamon
1 teaspoon ras-el-hanout
**600 ml (1 pint) seafood stock (see
page 183)**
**1 small preserved lemon,
finely sliced**
**12 green Manzanilla olives, pitted
and halved**
**2 tablespoons roughly chopped
coriander**
**salt and freshly ground black
pepper**
sprigs of coriander, to garnish

TO SERVE
couscous

Sprinkle the fish with half of the ground cumin and season with pepper. Transfer to a bowl and refrigerate for 30 minutes or until required.

Heat the oil in a large, heatproof casserole. Add the remaining cumin and the onion, garlic, saffron, cinnamon, ras-el-hanout, stock and preserved lemon. Bring to the boil and simmer for 15–20 minutes or until the onion and lemon are soft and the liquid has reduced by half.

Add the monkfish to the sauce together with the olives and chopped coriander. Cook over a low heat for 3–4 minutes or until the fish is just cooked. Season to taste with salt and pepper and garnish with coriander sprigs. Serve the tagine directly from the casserole with couscous.

Try this with brill, turbot or add prawns

Gurnard

with Shiitake & Thyme en Papillotte

Serves 4

**4 whole gurnard, each about 400 g
(14 oz), prepared (see page 31)**
1 red onion, thinly sliced
**100 g (4 oz) shiitake mushrooms,
thickly sliced**
juice of ½ lemon
8 sprigs of thyme
splash of extra virgin olive oil
**salt and freshly ground black
pepper**

TO SERVE
splash of truffle oil
rocket leaves or sprigs of watercress

Try this with red mullet
or John Dory

Preheat the oven to 220°C/425°F/gas mark 7. Preheat 2 baking sheets. Cut 4 heart shapes from pieces of good-quality greaseproof paper about 60 cm (24 in) long and fold them in half to crease the centre line.

Put a gurnard on one side of each piece of greaseproof paper. Sprinkle the red onion and mushrooms over the top of each fish. Splash a little lemon juice over the top and add the sprigs of thyme. Drizzle with a little olive oil and season with salt and pepper.

Wrap the fish carefully, taking care that the paper is sealed well (like a Cornish pasty) but that there is still room for steam to circulate around the fish. Lift the paper parcels on to the hot baking sheets and cook in the oven for 12–15 minutes or until a metal skewer inserted through the paper and into the fish comes out piping hot after 20 seconds.

Lift the parcels on to individual dinner plates and allow each guest to open at the table and enjoy the freshly opened aroma of the fish and herbs.

Sprinkle 2–3 drops of truffle oil over the fish at the table and serve with a simple rocket or watercress leaf salad.

A Day at
the Market

Once inside Billingsgate, you'll discover a virtual microcosm of society with its own rules and hierarchy. This is what makes the market so enduring and also so cloaked in history and tradition. Everyone is aware of their place and the boundaries that can and cannot be crossed. However, it can be slightly baffling to the outsider and is as much a lesson in sociology as a shopping experience. The merchants trade an equal amount of fish and banter, voices vying for attention above the constant din of market life. Porters push trolleys piled high with boxes of fish as unwary bystanders duck and dive to one side to avoid them. Customers inspect, peruse, prod and haggle. The floor glistens more as the morning progresses and steam from the ice rises and mingles with steam from hot drinks. Tonnes of ice are needed to keep the fish cool while gallons of hot drinks are produced in the cafe to keep the merchants and porters warm on chilly days.

Early Start

Although trading can't officially begin until 4.45am, most of the merchants arrive a few hours before this. The only thing that signifies a typical day is the fact that Billingsgate merchants start work well before dawn. There's plenty to do before the stands open for business. In fact, the market never really sleeps as deliveries arrive all through the night with lorries unloading the precious cargo that could have travelled to Billingsgate from anywhere in the world. Billingsgate offers the widest selection of fish and shellfish in the UK and on any given day there could be between 150 and 200 different varieties available to buy.

Fish is stored in the purpose built cold stores and the merchants take stock of deliveries, check supplies and finalise any phone orders before the sun has even thought about making an

appearance. Many of the Merchants' bigger orders will be placed over the phone and it's not unusual for companies to buy a huge quantity of fish that will never see the inside of Billingsgate market. Specialist transport companies operate out of the major ports and airports, handling orders directly and liaising with the Merchants over the phone. The fish is loaded straight onto the vans and delivered to the customers. This actually has the benefit of keeping precious space free at the market and it also cuts down on food miles and transport costs.

By 3.30am the market floor begins to fill up with porters, either dashing around to get the stands stocked with fish, or waiting to be booked for the day by a merchant who needs extra help. By now the market is really buzzing and the volume gradually increases as everyone tries to make themselves heard and get their stands ready for the start of the business day. By 4.30am the noise crescendos and an air of expectancy hangs over the market hall. The two cafés at Billingsgate operate throughout the night and provide the workers with hot drinks and a wide selection of food. Always worth a visit, you can catch up on the gossip and receive a warm welcome in both – and be sure of a wide variety of breakfast offerings to boot.

The Bells

At 4.45am the first bell rings and the porters can then begin serving the merchants. Only inter-trading is allowed at this stage; that is, merchants trading fish amongst themselves. The bell is followed by a flurry of activity and a further volume increase as the porters make mad dashes around the market hall, ferrying boxes of fish between merchants as quickly as possible. Any clumsily placed foot or limb is liable to come into contact with

  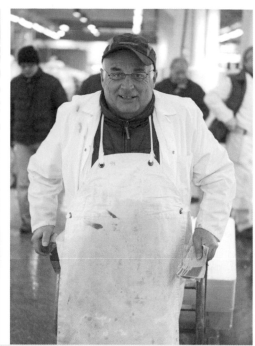

a fast moving porter's trolley at this stage of the day and the apology will be expected from the injured party. It's crucial that this part of trading is completed as quickly as possible so that public trading can begin.

There are just 15 brief minutes in which to complete the bulk of these deals. Then, at 5am, the second bell lets the merchants and porters know that they can now begin selling to the public. As Billingsgate shuts up shop for the day before the majority of shops are even open, the selling is mainly concentrated into a couple of frenetic hours. During this time, wholesalers, restaurateurs, café owners and members of the public trudge along the damp floor and go shopping for fish. If anyone's still feeling a bit bleary eyed as they walk in from the dark, the glare of the lights, the din of a couple of hundred raised voices and the inevitable smell of fish should banish any yearnings for the duvet and pyjamas. Billingsgate is truly an assault on all the senses and, as soon as you walk through the door, it wakes you up like a sharp slap round the face or the buzz of a double espresso.

Billingsgate is truly an assault on all the senses

Some customers visit the same merchants every time and dash in and out in a matter of minutes. They know exactly what they want to buy and where they want to buy it. They might take a look at the sample boxes on display and then place their order based on the quality of the sample. Once purchased, the porter will collect the fish from the cold store and take it out to the customer's van. Other visitors prefer to take their time and browse: either looking for what's good on that particular day or walking around each stand until something catches their eye. They might be a little overawed if it's their first time at the market. The rules are simple and the etiquette is inferred, however, any new situation can be a baffling one and a bustling fish market is certainly a very different shopping experience to a supermarket.

Law and Order

Even when Billingsgate is at its busiest it's easy to recognise the officials wandering round amongst the customers. Two distinct professions with two distinct uniforms, the Fisheries Inspectors and the Market Constables, are on hand before, during and after trading hours. They ensure the market runs smoothly, the customers are happy and the fish sold is in prime condition. An Inspector will generally take a tour around the market hall early on in the morning to ensure that stock is fresh. Constables make rounds in the market throughout the day, as well as checking the traffic flow outside. This includes customer vehicles, as well as delivery trucks, and certain times on certain days are particularly hectic. Saturday is the busiest day in terms of customers, as this is

the big day for the general public to visit Billingsgate. This means extra Constables on duty both inside and outside the market hall, as congestion builds and the 13-acre site bulges with people and vehicles. In terms of deliveries, Tuesday is the busiest day. With the market closed on Sundays and Mondays, Tuesday is the day for stocking up the cold stores and re-supplying the stands. Again, this means extra work for the Market Constables who must ensure that traffic keeps moving and tempers don't get frayed.

End of the Day

By about 8am trade begins to slow and the pace in the market hall shifts down a gear. Whilst there might still be a few customers milling around, most of the serious buyers have long since gone, many aiming to get through London before the congestion charge starts and their fish consignment gets a little bit pricier. As the final customers drift off, the full scale of the clean-up operation is visible and the momentous task of cleaning the stands and the hall begins in earnest.

Any unsold stock is taken back to the cold stores and the merchants tot up the day's sales in order to work out their orders for the following day. This is where the skill of a good merchant really becomes apparent. Not only do they have to estimate the stock that will be required over the following days, they must also take into account the weather, holiday periods, seasons and religious festivals – all of these can have a dramatic effect on supply and demand. There is such a delicate balance to be achieved between keeping sufficient stock and over-ordering. Too much stock could result in big losses, whilst too little could result in disgruntled customers, or customers buying from another merchant. Fresh fish has a very finite shelf life and if it remains unsold for more than a couple of days, it will have to be destroyed. A merchant's livelihood relies heavily on this ability to accurately predict requirements. There is also an element of uncertainty when it comes to the source of the supply. Whilst the demand might be there, the fish might not. Adverse weather conditions can change the nature of the market overnight: if the fish can't be caught or brought ashore, it can't be transported to market. As the merchants process all this information and work through their estimates, calculations and orders, the cleaners remove all signs of market activity for another day, leaving empty stands and freshly washed floors. By lunchtime the market hall is eerily quiet, a complete contrast to just a few hours' earlier. The empty space looks naked and incomplete, as if it's just biding its time until the early hours when the cycle begins once more.

By lunchtime the market hall is eerily quiet, a complete contrast to just a few hours' earlier

Plaice, Lemon sole, Dabs, Dover sole, Halibut, Turbot & Brill

What's on offer

There is always a large selection of flat fish available on the market. All of these fish have white texture, low fat flesh and include Dover sole, lemon sole, plaice, dabs, farmed and wild halibut, wild and farmed turbot and brill. Other flat species including witch and megrim are also occasionally available.

Plaice, Lemon Sole and Dabs

It is quite common to see fresh plaice and other small flat species, including dabs, on the market, that are still stiff with rigor mortis. This in an indication that the fish has been out of water for no more than thirty six to forty eight hours.

Plaice is sold whole, filleted or frozen and can be bought both as fillets and breaded. Plaice come from the UK coastline but also as far afield as Iceland. They are readily identifiable by their spots which are usually orange or rusty brown/green in colour if from Icelandic water.

Lemon sole is a close relative of plaice. They have a delicate flavour and it is one of the best of the smaller flat fish available. These fish have a mottled sandy brown skin and are distinguished by a small 'piping' of yellow around the gill flap on the head – the body is also lemon shaped.

FROM TOP TO BOTTOM: Lemon sole, turbot and Dover sole.

Lemon sole and dabs are used at the school, depending on the availability of the fish. Flat fish are not always at their best eating quality during the spawning season, which takes place in winter and early spring. When the roe develops there is less flesh and the effort of spawning means the fillets of the fish can be thin and watery. It is possible to tell when a flat fish is full of roe as it can usually be seen where the fish has been gutted.

On our courses we show how to trim the fins, take off the head and clean away the blood line (see page 27). Although we always look at filleting these fish we often recommend that they are cooked whole. Not only is it easier to cook fish well on the bone as it doesn't dry out so readily, but the bones contribute to the flavour of the overall fish.

Dover Sole

Dover sole is one of the most popular and often expensive fish on the market. The fish is traditionally served on the bone and a fishmonger will usually offer to skin it due to the impalatable nature of the skin that is as rough as a cat's tongue. The flesh is dense and well-flavoured and is best baked, grilled or pan-fried. We use this fish at the school when it is not full of roe or spawning. We show how to trim and skin the fish, remove the head and how to locate the blood line of the fish. This needs to be removed as it tastes bitter.

Halibut

Both Atlantic and a small quantity of Pacific halibut species are available at the market. Halibut is the largest of all the flat fish and can be identified by its diamond shaped body and large tail. You can't miss them as a large whole fish is spectacular to look at. The flesh of a halibut is white and flaky with a delicate flavour. Many merchants sell it on the market – both wild and farmed halibut are available. It is mainly sold whole, but some companies sell it ready prepared in steaks and, on occasions, frozen. It is a premium fish and fetches a high price.

A whole fish is usually displayed white belly side up to enable you to see the colour of the creamy white skin. This can be an indicator of quality, but will also give you an idea if the fish as been farmed or is wild. Wild fish will have a pure white belly, but the white skin of a farmed fish can have a mottled appearance. With a whole fish the size will vary quite dramatically. All flat fish have a generous covering of slime and on a fresh specimen this should be clear. Farmed halibut often has an inky coloured slime that is quite normal.

Halibut has a delicate white texture that tastes best when served simply. Pan-frying, char-grilling, grilling or steaming are all excellent methods of cooking this fish. We use farmed halibut at the school to demonstrate steaking of a large flat fish. A halibut can be prepared in a variety of ways. A small fish can be filleted like any other flat fish – into four quarter fillets for a chef or two cross cut fillets for a fishmonger. A large fish would usually be cut widthways across the body into thick steaks – for this you will need a steaking knife and a mallet to help cut through the central bone.

Turbot and Brill

The most prized of the flat fish is turbot, which is round in shape with sharp tubecules on the skin. Often referred to as the 'king of fish', it has a very firm meaty texture that doesn't break up easily and therefore can be stir-fried. It is available both farmed and wild. Brill is not as meaty as turbot but is considered by many to have more flavour. Brill is closely related to turbot and the two can be confused. Brill has a smooth skin and an oval shaped body. It is usually up to a third cheaper than turbot.

"Lemon sole is great baked in the oven in tin foil with a bit of lemon juice. I like eating it with salad and bread & butter – it's gotta be white bread though." **Colin, porter**

Simple, Plaice Supper

Serves 2

2 baking potatoes, thinly sliced
1 onion, finely sliced
25 g (1 oz) melted butter
4 sprigs of thyme
1 lemon, cut into 6 wedges
salt and freshly ground black pepper
2 small plaice, each about 450 g (1 lb), heads off, trimmed and blood line removed (see page 27)

Try this with small whole trout

Preheat the oven to 200°C/400°F/gas mark 6.

Put the potatoes and onion in the bottom of a large roasting tin, drizzle with melted butter, add the thyme, lemon wedges and season generously with salt and pepper. Toss everything together so that the vegetables are well coated in both the butter and seasoning. Spread flat into a single layer in the roasting tin and bake in the oven for 20 minutes.

When the potatoes are nearly cooked arrange the fish on top of the potatoes and season lightly. Return to the oven for 20–25 minutes or until the fish is cooked; the skin will lift away and the flesh will be opaque and white.

Transfer the fish to 2 serving plates, spoon the potatoes, onions and lemon over the top and serve immediately.

Pan-fried Flat Fish with Anchovy & Balsamic Glaze

Serves 4

4 large flat white fish fillets
1 onion, finely chopped
15 g (½ oz) butter
2 tablespoons thyme leaves
1 tablespoon balsamic vinegar
2 anchovy fillets
75 g (3 oz) unsalted butter

Try this with monkfish fillets

Skin the fillets and set aside.

Cook the onion in 15 g (½ oz) butter until very soft, drain and allow the butter to cool. Put the softened onion with the thyme, balsamic vinegar and anchovy fillets in a food processor and whiz together until well chopped. Add the unsalted butter and pulse the machine on and off until the well mixed.

Melt a little of the flavoured butter in a frying pan, add the fish and pan-fry for 1–2 minutes on each side until the fish is cooked. Transfer to serving plates. Melt more butter in the pan and spoon over the fish to serve.

Flat Fish
with Prawns & Pesto

Serves 4

FOR THE PESTO
small handful of basil leaves
small handful of chopped parsley
50 g (2 oz) Parmesan cheese,
    freshly grated
2 cloves garlic, crushed
5 tablespoons extra virgin olive oil
50 g (2 oz) toasted pine nuts
2 anchovy fillets

8 quarter-cross fillets of flat fish,
    such as dab or plaice
splash of olive oil
250 g (9 oz) cooked North Atlantic
    prawns, peeled
splash of extra virgin olive oil

TO GARNISH
lemon wedges
sprigs of basil

Make the pesto. Put the basil, parsley, Parmesan and garlic into a food processor. Whiz together until well chopped, add the olive oil, pine nuts, anchovies and pulse on and off until well mixed. Set aside until required.

Preheat the oven to 200°C/400°F/gas mark 6. Skin the fish and place the fillets, skinned side up, on a chopping board. Arrange the peeled prawns on the fish, spoon some pesto on top of each fillet and fold the fillets into 3 to make parcels.

Place the fish in an ovenproof dish, drizzle with some olive oil and bake in the oven for 12–15 minutes or until cooked; the flesh will be opaque and flaky. Garnish with lemon wedges and sprigs of basil and serve immediately.

"I don't like 'fishy-fish', but brill simply baked in foil with bay leaves is fantastic and often served at Maggie's, my mother-in-law's restaurant."

Chris Gill, porter, Barton & Hart

Dover Sole

with Wild Mushrooms, Sage & Crème Fraîche

Serves 2

**2 Dover sole, each about 450 g
(1 lb), skinned, heads removed
and trimmed
25 g (1 oz) butter
1 small clove garlic, chopped
75 g (3 oz) wild mushrooms, such as
chanterelles and morels
2 teaspoons chopped sage
4 tablespoons half-fat crème fraîche
2 tablespoons fresh breadcrumbs
½ tablespoon freshly grated
Parmesan cheese
salt and freshly ground black
pepper**

Heat the oven to 200°C/400°F/gas mark 6. Working on the dark skinned side of the fillet, make an incision straight down the back of the fish until you hit the bone. Lift the fillets as if quarter-cross filleting, but leaving the fillets attached to the frill, just so they have been 'turned back' (see page 28). Transfer to a foil-lined baking sheet.

Meanwhile, melt the butter in a frying pan. Add the garlic and mushrooms and stir-fry over a medium to high heat for 2–3 minutes. Stir in the sage and crème fraîche and remove from the heat. Season to taste with salt and pepper.

Spoon the mushroom mixture into the centre of the fish and sprinkle with the breadcrumbs and cheese. Bake in the oven for 10–12 minutes or until the breadcrumbs are lightly toasted and the fish fillets are opaque. Serve immediately.

Try this with small whole trout

"I like Dover sole grilled and served with mashed potato. No fancy sauces though, just lemon and pepper."

Don Tyler, J. Bennett Jnr.

Lemon Sole
with Roast Tomato, Basil & Parmesan

Serves 2

2 small whole lemon sole, filleted
salt and freshly ground black
  pepper
4 small tomatoes, halved
1 tablespoon pine nuts
1 tablespoon extra virgin olive oil
1 tablespoon freshly grated
  Parmesan cheese
1 tablespoon freshly shredded basil
1 tablespoon balsamic vinegar

Heat the oven to 200°C/400°F/gas mark 6.

Skin the fish and lightly season the skinned side of each fillet and fold into 3 to make small parcels. Transfer the fish to an oven-to-table roasting dish and tuck the tomatoes around the sides. Sprinkle with the pine nuts, olive oil, pepper and Parmesan.

Roast in the oven for 10–12 minutes or until the tomatoes are beginning to soften but not break up and the fish is cooked; it will be opaque and flaky.

Sprinkle the top of the roast with basil and balsamic vinegar. Serve straight from the roasting dish.

Lemon Sole
Gratin

Serves 4

3 large lemon sole, filleted
2 tablespoons olive oil
pinch of grated nutmeg
1 clove garlic, crushed
salt and freshly ground black
  pepper
150 g (5 oz) spinach, washed
3 tablespoons grated Gruyère
  cheese
2 tablespoons fresh breadcrumbs

Preheat the oven to 200°C/400°F/gas mark 6. Skin the fillets and set aside.

Heat the olive oil in a large frying pan, add the nutmeg, garlic and seasoning. Add the spinach and toss over a high heat for 1 minute or until the spinach wilts. Tip on to a plate to cool.

Mix the cheese and breadcrumbs together and season lightly.

Arrange the cool spinach on the fillets and fold each fillet into 3 to encase the spinach. Arrange in a large dish and sprinkle over the cheese crumb mixture.

Bake in the oven for 12–15 minutes or until the fish is cooked; it should be white opaque and firm to the touch. Serve immediately.

Turbot & Scallop Bisque

Serves 6

400 g (14 oz) turbot fillets, skinned
8 scallops
500 kg (1¼ lb) rope-grown mussels
1 squid, prepared (see page 39)
8 tiger prawns, peeled
olive oil, for frying

FOR THE BISQUE SAUCE
½ onion, sliced
1 clove garlic, chopped
bouquet garni
100 ml (3½ fl oz) dry white wine
100 ml (3½ fl oz) water
15 g (½ oz) butter or 1 tablespoon
    olive oil
1 teaspoon tomato purée
1 leek, white part only, thinly sliced
400 ml (14 fl oz) seafood stock
    (see page 183)
150 ml (5 fl oz) crème fraîche
salt and freshly ground black
    pepper
1 tablespoon finely chopped parsley
blanched needle shreds of the green
    part of the leek, to garnish

TO SERVE
mashed potatoes

A classic bisque is a rich shellfish soup. This recipe uses stock to make a creamy, bisque-style reduction that can be served with many types of seafood.

Prepare the fish. Cut the turbot into 5 cm (2 in) pieces and chill. Open the scallops with a knife and lift from the shell. Remove the frill and stomach sac to reveal the white muscle and roe or coral, rinse and pat dry. Wash and debeard the mussels. Check for signs of life: the mussels should be closed. If open, tap sharply and if they don't close discard. Discard any that are cracked or broken. Cut the squid into strips and devein the prawns.

Make the sauce. Put the onion, garlic, bouquet garni, wine and water into a large saucepan, bring to the boil and simmer for 2–3 minutes. Add the mussels only, cover and cook for 3–4 minutes or until they are steamed open. Transfer the mussels to a plate and discard any that have not opened. Strain the cooking liquor into a bowl. Lift the mussels from the shells, keeping a few in their shells for garnish. Set the mussels aside.

Melt the butter or heat the oil in a large, clean saucepan, add the tomato purée and stir for 1 minute. Add the leek and cook for a further 3–4 minutes or until softened. Add the stock and reserved cooking liquor from the mussels and bring to the boil. Simmer for 4–5 minutes or until reduced by half. Whisk in the crème fraîche, bring to the boil and simmer for a further few minutes or until creamy in consistency. Carefully season to taste and stir in the parsley.

Add the turbot to the bisque and poach over a low heat for 3–4 minutes or until cooked and the fish is opaque. Add the shelled mussels and heat through thoroughly. Pan-fry the scallops and prawns in a little very hot olive oil on either side until just cooked and sear the prepared squid for a few seconds until opaque. Add to the bisque and remove from the heat.

Spoon the fish and some sauce on to warm plates and garnish with leek needle shreds. Serve with mashed potato.

Turbot
with Capers & Parsley Beurre Noisette

Serves 2

2 turbot fillets, skinned
2 tablespoons plain flour seasoned with salt and pepper
40 g (1½ oz) butter
1 tablespoon extra virgin olive oil
1 tablespoon capers
1 tablespoon chopped parsley
1 tablespoon chopped sage
juice of ½ lemon

TO SERVE
small splash of truffle oil

Roll the fillets in the seasoned flour and shake to remove the excess. Lay them in a single layer on a plate until you are ready to cook.

Melt half of the butter in a large frying pan, add the olive oil and heat until the butter has stopped sizzling and has just begun to brown. Add half the fish and fry for 1–2 minutes on each side. Transfer to a serving dish and fry the second batch of fish. Keep the fish warm.

Wipe the frying pan with absorbent kitchen paper and add the remaining butter. Heat until it begins to brown and add the capers, herbs and lemon juice. The liquid will bubble up. Shake over the heat for a few seconds, and while it is still sizzling pour the liquid over the fish. Splash with truffle oil to serve.

Try this with ray, halibut or trout

Grilled Halibut
with Gremolata Gruyère Crumb
Serves 4

50 g (2 oz) Gruyère cheese, grated
3 tablespoons fresh breadcrumbs
1 tablespoon chopped parsley
grated zest of 1 lemon
4 halibut fillets or steaks
15 g (½ oz) butter, melted
salt and freshly ground black
**   pepper**

TO SERVE
flat leaf parsley
lemon wedges

This simple dish demonstrates how quickly fish cooks under the grill. You can use any species of white fish with this recipe, particularly members of the flat fish family. If the fish is a single fillet and no more than 1 cm (½ in) deep it may need grilling on one side only. If this is the case grill the fish for a minute, then sprinkle with the crumb and finish under the grill until the fish is cooked.

Preheat the grill to its highest setting.

Mix together the cheese, breadcrumbs, parsley and lemon zest, season lightly and set aside.

Put the halibut on a baking sheet, brush with melted butter and season lightly with salt and pepper. Grill the fish for 2–3 minutes on one side. Turn over if necessary (see above) and sprinkle the second side of the fish with the crumb mixture.

Return to the grill and cook for a further 3–4 minutes or until the crumb is golden-brown and the fish cooked. Garnish with parsley and lemon wedges and serve.

Pan-fried Halibut
with Puttanesca-style Dressing

Serves 4

4 halibut steaks
3 tablespoons plain flour seasoned
  with salt and pepper
25 g (1 oz) butter
1 tablespoon olive oil

FOR THE DRESSING
4 red peppers, grilled, seeded
  and skins removed
2 tablespoons extra virgin olive oil
225 g (8 oz) cherry tomatoes, halved
12 pitted Kalamata olives
2 tablespoons capers, drained and
  roughly chopped
2 tablespoons shredded basil
salt and freshly ground black
  pepper

Prepare the dressing. Thickly slice the red peppers. Heat the olive oil in a pan and add the tomatoes. Cook over a low heat for 2–3 minutes or until they begin to soften, Stir in the peppers, olives, capers and basil, warm through and season to taste.

Roll the halibut steaks in seasoned flour. Heat the butter and olive oil together in a large frying pan until the butter stops sizzling, add the fish and pan-fry for 3–5 minutes on each side or until the fish is cooked; it will look opaque and be firm to the touch and golden-brown. (For a lighter option, brush the halibut with a little olive oil, season and grill for 2–3 minutes on each side.)

Arrange the fish on a large platter and spoon the dressing over the top to serve.

"You can't beat a nice halibut steak with root vegetables. First slice any root vegetables you like and put into a dish. Splash over some white wine and stock, cover tightly with foil and put in the oven for 20 minutes. Then place the halibut steak on top of the vegetables, add a knob of butter and some pepper and put back in the oven until cooked."

Dave Aldous, porter

Tuna, Mackerel, King Fish & related species

Mackerel

You can't beat Billingsgate mackerel! It is a wonderful inexpensive fish, oil rich and high in omega 3. Mackerel is at its best when as fresh as possible and much of the fish available at Billingsgate reaches the market quickly so that it is either stiff with rigor mortis or very firm. This is an indicator that the fish has been out of the water for only a few hours. Good quality mackerel will have lovely glossy skin, bright eyes and deep red gills and is likely to have a subtle aroma of sea ozone.

Coming from a variety of sources and available whole, fresh and frozen as well as in fillets and smoked, this fish requires minimal preparation and many merchants sell it. The cost of this fish makes it an excellent choice to buy by the box to take home for the barbecue. Several different methods are used to catch mackerel and at the school we prefer to use line caught if available. Fish from Scotland and Cornwall are available. Scottish mackerel have a higher oil content making them perfect for smoking, whereas Cornish tends to be leaner, but just as fabulous.

If the fish is still 'round' (meaning ungutted) all you need to do is remove the head and slit the belly and remove the guts. If you want to leave the head on also remove the gills. Once gutted take care to rinse the belly of the fish to remove the 'blood line', this runs close to the back bone of the fish and can be very bitter to taste (see page 33). Once prepared take care to keep the fish very cold and enjoy it as soon as you can. Although all fish needs very careful handling and chilling, members of this group of fish need to be kept at a low and constant temperature.

We use this fish at the school for teaching basic gutting and cleaning, removing gills and, if required, how to take the head off ensuring maximum yield. Fresh mackerel is best grilled, roasted or barbecued and the flavour of the flesh is such that it takes robust flavours including chilli, ginger, spices, soy and sesame

well, although it is traditionally served accompanied by a simple gooseberry sauce with a hint of ginger. The skin is delicate and therefore it is difficult to pan-fry this fish successfully as the skin sticks to the frying pan.

Tuna & King Fish

Tuna is the largest member of the family and is related to mackerel. There is a selection of tuna family members available at the market, from large yellow fin tuna to smaller skipjack, bought to the market from various sources and caught by various methods. Pole caught is a responsible way of catching tuna as it minimizes bycatch.

At the school we purchase yellow-fin tuna and, as it can be a large fish, always pre-cut as a loin. The loin (which is the leanest cut of the fish) is sold vacuum-packed and a label will indicate not only the common and Latin names but also when it was processed. The loin is also available wrapped in muslin (then vacuum packed) which is sold as 'sashimi grade' tuna and it is slightly more costly. It has a meaty texture and, if cooked when very fresh, is the nearest fish alternative to beef steak.

Choose tuna loins that have a deep claret colour as when the fish loses condition the meat begins to turn brown and some of the flavour is lost. We simply cut the loin into steaks for either pan-frying or griddling. As tuna loin is such good value we often cut it and then freeze the steaks individually for up to a month, and have found it to hold up well under these conditions.

CLOCKWISE FROM TOP LEFT: Scad, mackerel, melva (frigate mackerel), king fish, sprats (in bowl).

Another member of this group, Melva (or frigate mackerel) is also available, as is bonito. These are sold whole and, like all the tuna member group, have a bullet shaped body. These particular fish have dark red meaty flesh, which, like mackerel, is very well suited to robust flavours including soy, sesame and chilli. Once prepared they have no bones and are a good 'first try' fish for those who enjoy meat but are not keen on fish due to the bones.

King fish (or king mackerel) is the long and lean member of the tuna group and an impressive sight. It comes from a variety of sources, but is a warm water species. It is available at the market, both fresh and frozen, and currently is a good choice for exotic fish recipes.

Scad

These fish are smaller than mackerel, but similarly are often still stiff with rigor mortis when sold at the market. In a very fresh state they have bright black eyes with glistening skin. On close inspection they have a row of small protruding scutes along the flank that are best removed before serving. Their delicate oily flesh that is less rich than mackerel, but can be used as an alternative.

Sousing is a very traditional method of making the most of some species of fish, particularly oil-rich. Mackerel and herring are often used, but the subtlety of the sousing spices work well with scad. There are many recipes for pickling this type of fish and this would date back to times when a large catch would need to be preserved for a fishing community during lean months. Rollmops usually spring to mind, but sousing is a great alternative.

Herring & Sardines

Herrings and sardines are excellent value for money and brimming with omega 3. Fresh herrings from around both the UK and Norway are available at various times of the year. Thames herring are a particular treat and are certified by the MSC. English herrings tend to be smaller and are used extensively for smoking as a kipper. Norwegian herrings are usually the larger and more abundant of the two and have a richer, oilier texture. Available

by the box at the market and usually stiff with rigor mortis, they are always an inexpensive purchase and great for a brunch or barbeque. It is a beautiful looking fish with loose scales, beady black eyes and gleaming silvery skin. Closely related to sardines, the two species can be confused.

Sardines are also available from a variety of sources. Small fish are sold as sardines and larger ones sold as pilchards. Both these fish should be enjoyed as fresh as possible, so look for rigor mortis when buying.

When buying these species for use at the school we find they are at their best scaled, gutted and rinsed and then cooked whole. Keep any roe that you find as this is particularly good – especially the soft roe, or milt. We use them for grilling or barbecuing and eaten as fresh as possible (fab for breakfast) the flavour is always delicate, although there are quite a few bones to contend with.

Sprats

A big box of very fresh sprats, still bright, rigid and practically winking at you, always enthuses anyone shopping around the market. Available both fresh, when in season, and hot smoked, these are always sold by the box and generally are excellent value for money. Like all other oil rich fish you can't enjoy these fresh enough. They are so delicate that they lose condition fairly quickly, but this makes them very easy to prepare. Run a small knife (or finger) along the belly to open them up, remove any innards and quickly rinse. The head can be removed if wished. Pat dry and then quickly toss in seasoned flour and quickly pan-fry – a plate of these for breakfast with a squeeze of lemon is a good start to the day! The merchants who sell them also enjoy them, too – a handful are sent to one of the café's on the market, who very willingly cook them up and deliver them to the offices on the first floor at the end of trading. They are considered to be quite bony, but can be boned by gutting, pressing a finger along the spine to loosen the bone and then pulling the head and main bone away. We use this technique for the Cured Sprat recipe on page 112 – buy a 'stone' box (6.36 kg), use some pan-fried for breakfast and cure the remainder. Despite the preparation required, you are unlikely to regret it.

Oatmeal Herrings

with Bacon   Serves 4

8 small herrings, gutted
50 g (2 oz) medium oatmeal
4 rashers of streaky bacon
2 tablespoons olive oil
splash of lemon juice
salt and freshly ground black
    pepper

TO SERVE
soda bread

Try this with mackerel
or sardines

Herring contains high levels of omega 3, the health benefits of which are widely documented. Billingsgate sells some of the best and freshest herrings available, and they have often been out of water for only a few hours.

Rinse the herrings and pat them dry. Dip in the oatmeal and season lightly with salt and pepper. Set aside.

Fry the bacon in a large frying pan until the fat runs and the bacon is crisp. Transfer the bacon to a plate and keep warm. Heat the oil in the pan, add the herrings and pan-fry for 2–3 minutes on each side until the fish is cooked. The fish will feel firm to the touch and the eye will be white.

Transfer the herrings to a serving dish, sprinkle with a little lemon juice and arrange the bacon on top. Serve with soda bread.

"We eat fish twice a week in my house, and when I was a kid we ate it all weekend. My favourite dish is herrings wrapped in tin foil with a bay leaf and some lemon juice, cooked in the oven for 20 minutes and served with a salad." **Robin, J. Bennett**

Pan-fried
Herring Roe

Serves 2

on Toast with Capers
& Parsley

soft or hard roe from 4 herrings
2 tablespoons plain flour seasoned
   with salt and pepper
25 g (1 oz) butter
2 rounds of toasted wholemeal
   bread
2 tablespoons Worcestershire sauce
splash of lemon juice
1 tablespoon capers
1 tablespoon chopped flat leaf
   parsley
salt and freshly ground black
   pepper

It is traditional to serve soft roe on toast, but you can use hard roe if you prefer.

Roll the roe in the seasoned flour. Melt half of the butter in a large frying pan and heat until it is hot and foaming. Add the roe and pan-fry for 1–2 minutes, turning once; they are cooked when they feel firm to the touch. Lift on to the rounds of toast and keep warm.

Wipe the frying pan with absorbent kitchen paper, add the remaining butter and allow it to melt and just turn brown. Remove the pan from the heat and add the Worcestershire sauce, lemon juice, capers and parsley. Swirl around the pan and then season to taste with salt and pepper. Pour over the herring roe and serve hot.

Grilled Mackerel

with Soy & Sesame Baste   Serves 4

4 small mackerel, gutted
4 tablespoons dark soy sauce
2 teaspoons sesame oil
2 teaspoons honey
1 tablespoon sesame seeds
2.5 cm (1 in) piece of fresh root
    ginger, peeled and thinly sliced
freshly ground black pepper

TO SERVE
½ cucumber, thinly sliced
handful of coriander leaves
splash of rice wine vinegar

Try this with salmon
or herring

Few of us eat as much oil-rich fish as we should, but half a fillet of mackerel can contain the advised daily allowance of omega 3. We always try and include a recipe with mackerel, herring or sprats on all our courses, and Billingsgate mackerel are some of the freshest and best available.

Preheat the grill to its highest setting. Rinse the mackerel, taking care to remove the gills and clean out the blood line of the fish (this is close to the backbone and tastes bitter – see page 33).

In a bowl make the baste by mixing together the soy sauce, sesame oil, honey, sesame seeds and ginger. Season with pepper.

Make 5–6 slashes through the fish on each side of the fillets and then brush thoroughly with the baste. Push a piece of the ginger into each slit of the fish and arrange on a baking sheet.

Cook under the grill for 3–4 minutes on each side. The fish is cooked when the flesh is opaque, and the skin will be charred and shiny.

Arrange the cucumber slices on 4 plates, put the fish on top, sprinkle with some coriander leaves and splash with wine vinegar.

"At home we microwave mackerel with Italian plum tomatoes and a splash of balsamic vinegar – it's fabulous."

Barry O'Toole, Fisheries Inspector

Grilled Mackerel
with Almond & Cranberry Glaze

Serves 4

**4 small mackerel, filleted and
pin-boned (see page 38)**
olive oil, for brushing
**salt and freshly ground black
pepper**
watercress leaves, to garnish

FOR THE GLAZE
1 tablespoon olive oil
2 shallots, finely sliced
2 tablespoons balsamic vinegar
4 tablespoons cranberry sauce
**2 tablespoons flaked almonds,
toasted**

Mackerel is classically partnered with gooseberry sauce, in much the same way that pork and apple sauce go hand in glove. The acidity of cranberries also works well with mackerel as the tartness of the fruit cuts through the oily richness of the fish.

Preheat the grill to its highest setting.

Arrange the mackerel fillets, skin side up, on the grill tray. Lightly brush with oil and season lightly with salt and pepper.

Grill for 3–4 minutes or until the skin begins to blister and the flesh looks opaque and flaky.

Meanwhile, prepare the glaze. Heat the oil in a small saucepan, add the shallots and cook for 3–4 minutes or until soft. Add the balsamic vinegar and cranberry sauce, bring to the boil and season to taste with salt and pepper. Brush the mackerel with the glaze and sprinkle with the almonds. Arrange on a plate and serve garnished with watercress.

"Take a lovely mackerel bought fresh from the market and score it using a sharp knife. Slice up some peppers and tomatoes then push the peppers into the cuts in the flesh and the tomatoes into the cavity. Drizzle with olive oil – drizzle is a great word isn't it? I like that – then roast in the oven until cooked." **Ben, Bards Shellfish**

Smoked Paprika
King Fish Casserole
with Olives

Serves 4

4 king fish steaks, about 5 cm
   (2 in) thick
3 tablespoons plain flour seasoned
   with salt, pepper and 1 tablespoon
   smoked paprika
2 tablespoons olive oil
1 red pepper, thickly sliced
1 teaspoon tomato purée
2 teaspoons dark brown sugar
150 ml (5 fl oz) red Rioja
410 g (14½ oz) can chopped
   tomatoes
100 g (4 oz) pitted green olives
   (preferably Manzanilla)
1 tablespoon chopped sage
salt and freshly ground black
   pepper
4 tablespoons crème fraîche

Roll the fish in the seasoned flour, making sure that each piece is well coated.

Heat the oil in a large sauté pan. Add the fish and pan-fry on all sides for 3–4 minutes or until well browned. Transfer to a plate. Add the red pepper, tomato purée and sugar to the pan, stir over a medium heat for 2–3 minutes and then stir in the wine. Bring to the boil and simmer until the wine has reduced by a half. Return the fish to the pan and add the tomatoes. Bring to the boil, then reduce the heat and cook for 4–6 minutes or until the fish is cooked all the way through.

Lift the fish on to a serving dish, reduce the cooking liquid until syrupy. Add the green olives and sage and season to taste. Pour the sauce over the fish and spoon crème fraîche over the top to serve.

Try this with any firm textured or oil rich fish

Char-grilled Tuna
with Aubergine & Chilli Relish   Serves 2

2 yellow fin tuna steaks, each
about 150 g (5 oz)
1 tablespoon olive oil
salt and freshly ground black
pepper

FOR THE RELISH
1 aubergine
2 tablespoons extra virgin olive oil
1 red onion, finely sliced
2 cloves garlic, chopped
1–2 red chillies, seeded and finely
chopped
1 teaspoon honey
5 tablespoons white wine
5 tablespoons mirin
1 tablespoon dark soy sauce
salt and freshly ground black
pepper
2 tablespoons freshly chopped flat
leaf parsley
1 tablespoon freshly chopped mint
(optional)

Char-grilling is one of the best methods of cooking dense, meaty fish such as tuna. At the school we often serve a salsa or pesto with tuna, and this relish is particularly good.

Make the relish. Cut the aubergine into 2 cm (¾ in) dice, sprinkle with salt and leave to stand in a colander for 10 minutes.

Heat the oil in a large frying pan, add the onion and cook over a low heat for 3–4 minutes. Add the garlic, chilli and aubergine and cook for a further 5 minutes. Add the honey, white wine, mirin and soy sauce, bring to the boil and cook over a low heat until the aubergine is tender and the liquid has evaporated. Season to taste with salt and pepper and stir in the herbs.

Brush the tuna steaks with oil and season lightly with salt and plenty of pepper. Heat a griddle pan until it is beginning to smoke. Add the tuna and press on to the ridges of the pan. Sear for 1 minute, turn over and sear on the other side. Reduce the heat under the pan and continue to cook for a further 1–2 minutes on each side until the tuna has been cooked as required.

Transfer to serving plates and serve with the aubergine relish.

Pan-fried Sprats with Lemon

Serves 2

350 g (12 oz) sprats, gutted
3 tablespoons plain flour seasoned
with salt and pepper
1 tablespoon sunflower oil
25 g (1 oz) butter
splash of lemon juice
1 tablespoon chopped parsley

These simple sprats are delicious served with mashed potato or brown bread and butter.

Rinse the sprats and pat dry with absorbent kitchen paper. Toss the fish in the seasoned flour and arrange on a plate in a single layer so that they don't stick together.

Heat the oil in a large frying pan, then add the butter. When the butter has melted and has stopped sizzling add a handful of sprats in a single layer. Cook for 1 minute, then turn over and cook for a further minute on the second side. Transfer to a plate and keep warm while you cook the remaining fish. If the butter begins to look very brown, wipe the frying pan out with absorbent kitchen paper and replace with more oil and butter.

Pile the sprats on a serving dish, splash with lemon juice, sprinkle the chopped parsley on the top and serve immediately.

Soused Scad

4 scad, mackerel or herring, filleted
and pin-boned (see page 38)
salt and freshly ground black
pepper
150 ml (5 fl oz) distilled malt vinegar
mixed with 150 ml (5 fl oz) water
2 onions, thinly sliced
2 bay leaves
1 tablespoon pickling spices
1 teaspoon black peppercorns

TO SERVE
watercress salad
bread and butter

Sousing is a fantastic way of cooking herring, mackerel and scad.

Preheat the oven to 150°C/300°F/gas mark 2.

Lay the fish fillets, skin side down, on a board. Season with salt and pepper and roll up the fillets from the thick end to the tail end. Pack into an ovenproof dish. Pour the vinegar and water mixture over the top and add the onions, bay leaves, pickling spices and peppercorns.

Cover the dish with foil and bake in the oven for 1¼ hours. Leave to cool, then serve with a watercress salad and brown bread and butter.

Cured Sprats
with Beetroot & Mustard Dressing

Serves 4 (as a starter)

250 g (9 oz) fresh sprats
1 tablespoon sea salt
300 ml (10 fl oz) sherry or
   white wine vinegar
4 sprigs of thyme

FOR THE SALAD
4 tablespoons extra virgin olive oil
2 teaspoons French mustard
1 tablespoon balsamic vinegar
salt and freshly ground black
   pepper
2 large cooked beetroot, peeled and
   coarsely grated
1 red onion, finely sliced
1 tablespoon freshly chopped
   parsley

Sprats are easy to bone. Simply cut off the head and remove the guts. Run your thumb along the backbone inside the cavity to release the bone and gently ease it away.

Gut and bone the sprats. Wash and pat dry.

Arrange the fish in a single layer in a shallow dish, sprinkle with sea salt and pour over the vinegar and add the sprigs of thyme. Cover and refrigerate for 12 hours, preferably overnight.

The following day drain away and discard the vinegar. Pat the sprats dry with absorbent kitchen paper.

Prepare the salad. Put the oil, mustard and vinegar in a bowl and season lightly with salt and pepper. Whisk together to form an emulsion.

Toss the sprats with the beetroot, red onion and parsley and season to taste. Pile on a large serving plate, drizzle over the dressing and serve.

Try this with small herring

Mackerel

with Herby Couscous Stuffing
Serves 4

8 small mackerel fillets,
  pin-boned only

1 tablespoon extra virgin olive oil

2 teaspoons ground cumin

2 teaspoons ground coriander

2 teaspoons paprika

150 g (5 oz) couscous, about
  400 g (14 oz) when cooked

300 ml (10 fl oz) vegetable stock

grated zest of 1 lemon and splash
  of juice

2 tablespoons chopped coriander

2 tablespoons chopped parsley

25 g (1 oz) butter

salt and freshly ground black
  pepper

TO SERVE
lemon wedges

Spices work well with mackerel, as do sesame and soy. This spicy couscous is a wonderful and balanced filling that complements the richness of the mackerel.

Preheat the oven to 200°C/400°F/gas mark 6. Lay the mackerel fillets on a chopping board and season lightly with salt and pepper. Keep in the refrigerator until ready to use.

Heat the oil in a large saucepan, add the spices and fry for 30 seconds. Add the couscous and stir together until the grains are coated in the oil. Add the stock, bring to the boil and cook for a few minutes or until the couscous has swollen and is tender. Add the lemon zest, a splash of juice to taste and the herbs. Season to taste with salt and pepper. Tip on to a plate and leave to cool.

When it is cool spoon the couscous mixture on to the mackerel. Roll up the fillets and pack them neatly into a gratin dish, adding any extra couscous around the fish. Dot the top with butter and bake in the oven for 12–15 minutes or until the fish is cooked and the couscous crisp. Serve with lemon wedges.

Barbecued Scad with Summer Herb Salad

Serves 4

12 scad, scaled and gutted (see page 37)
2 tablespoons extra virgin olive oil
½ teaspoon ground coriander
salt and freshly ground black pepper

FOR THE SALAD
1 bunch of flat leaf parsley, leaves only, washed and roughly chopped
90 g (3½ oz) bag of salad leaves, including rocket and watercress leaves
2 spring onions, finely sliced
grated zest and juice of ½ lemon
3 tablespoons extra virgin olive oil
1 teaspoon Dijon mustard
½ teaspoon clear honey
2 teaspoons chopped oregano

Heat the barbecue until the coals are glowing red and the flames have died down, or alternatively heat the grill to its highest setting.

Brush the scad with olive oil and sprinkle with ground coriander and salt and pepper.

Prepare the salad. Toss the parsley leaves with the rocket and watercress and arrange on serving plates. Sprinkle over the spring onions. Put the lemon zest and juice in a small bowl, whisk in the olive oil, mustard and honey until well emulsified and add the oregano. Season to taste.

Cook the scad on the barbecue or under the grill for 1–2 minutes on each side until the skin is charred and the flesh has lost its translucency. Arrange on top of the salad and spoon the lemon dressing over the top. Serve immediately.

Try this with sardines or herring

Merchants & Porters

The fish at Billingsgate come in all shapes and sizes and from all corners of the globe. Whilst the people who work there might not relish being compared to the stock on sale, similarities are certainly there in terms of the rich diversity of professions, characters and backgrounds. Like the intricate mechanisms of a clock, market workers all perform their individual roles with a level of respect and understanding for other peoples' duties. This ensures that Billingsgate runs smoothly and efficiently.

The Show Must Go On

In some ways, the very layout of the market dictates the different professions and work environments and it could almost be likened to a theatre. Backstage the administration team keeps the show running on time, to schedule and with great efficiency. The Constables are on hand to check on everything front of house, while the Inspectors regulate the content. This leaves the merchants and porters to take centre stage in the Market Hall. And, like so many actors, they play their characters with aplomb. The difference between Billingsgate and a real theatre is that these characters are genuine. It's the merchants and porters who give the market its authenticity and help to make it a truly unique shopping experience. Whilst insults might be traded across the hall and orders shouted out with brusqueness, there's an underlying atmosphere of frivolity that seems to go hand-in-hand with the hard work and unsociable hours.

Career Ladder

As with many ancient London professions, the merchants and porters are a pretty tight-knit bunch and the tradition of working at the fish market tends to be passed down through the generations. This is particularly true of the porters and many of them have merely stepped into the shoes of their fathers, grandfathers and great-grandfathers as they continue the family tradition. In fact, as soon as you start talking to anyone on the market floor, you discover that any number of their relatives also work at Billingsgate. There are over 100 porters at the market but they don't all work there full-time. The full-time porters are attached to a particular trader and they will work solely for them, moving the boxes of fish between the cold store and the stand and taking it out to customers' vehicles. For this, the porters earn a basic salary. They then also receive a set amount for every stone of fish that they transport. This is called 'bobbin' money and relates to the fish brought out of the market. So, the wage can vary considerably, depending on how busy the merchant is and how efficiently the porter carries out their duties.

The remaining porters are casual workers. They're known as 'on the stones' or 'under the clock' porters, a term that refers to the beginning of their working day. Casual porters arrive early and congregate under the clock in the centre of the market hall, hoping to be taken on for a day's work by a busy merchant. If a regular porter calls in sick, or the merchant needs some extra help, they'll hire one of the casual porters. They can also be booked up in advance to cover holidays and particularly busy times at the market. Many of them, like Gary, carry a diary around in their back pocket so they can add in their working dates as and when a merchant books them.

> "I've worked on the market for 56 years and I've seen some changes in that time. I used to play football before I worked here – I played for England at the 1960 Olympics in Rome. I'm 72 now and you won't catch me retiring any time soon."
>
> **Terry, J.J. Ovenell**

Gary started working at Billingsgate after he left school at 16 and has clocked up an impressive 30 years as a casual porter. He's usually at the market by 3.45am and, if he doesn't have any work booked in the diary, he waits under the clock with the others. There's no guarantee of work for casual porters and most of them tend to have employment for an average of about eight months of the year. In such an uncertain work environment it makes sense to have a second income, which is why Gary and 11 other Billingsgate porters also own black cabs. The taxis are parked just outside the market and when his shift is over, he takes off his overalls and swaps the wheels of the fish trolley for the wheels of the cab. With City Airport and Docklands so close, there's always plenty of work just outside the market boundary. And it's not just cab driving that keeps the wages of the market porters topped up. There are also builders, welders, boxers and plasterers all slotting the different elements of their working lives together like a giant jigsaw. Whilst it wouldn't be viable to hold down a nine-to-five job as well as carrying out market porter duties, if you've got a trade or you work for yourself, it seems to be the ideal scenario.

The Merchants

A fish merchant has many roles and needs many talents to be successful at Billingsgate. Apart from the obvious knowledge of fish and the fish trade and the skewed body clock, they need to be personable, quick thinking, resilient and astute. The merchants lease their stands from the City of London. They pay a fixed contract, which includes cleaning and security costs, and the contract entitles them to trade from their premises in the market at the hours they choose. Merchants tend to arrive before the porters in the morning and they'll often be the last to leave the market floor after trading, just before the cleaners descend. It's a tough working life but if you speak to the merchants they'll

quickly tell you that they wouldn't have it any other way. It seems that Billingsgate is a very difficult habit to quit.

Someone who would wholeheartedly agree with this is Don, who runs J. Bennett Jnr. He originally qualified as an architect and was taking a couple of months off before his first job was due to start. His father ran the fish business at the time, at the old site, and he asked Don to help him out on the stand instead of sitting idly at home. Don never did take up the architect job and he eventually inherited the business from his father. There's another J. Bennett business at the market and although the two aren't linked now, they were originally set up by two brothers over 100 hundred years ago. Apparently, the brothers had a falling out and set up rival companies.

Keep it in the Family

A number of companies are family firms that have been passed down through the generations. However, there are others that have been inherited. It's not uncommon for an owner to leave their company to a favourite employee in order to carry on the name. This is one of the reasons that you'll find many businesses with names that have remained the same for hundreds of years but have no relevance to the people now working there. In some cases no one can remember who the original owner was but they wouldn't dream of changing the company name when they take it on. It seems to make perfect sense to carry on using the name with all its historical trading references.

Mike owns J. Nash & Sons Ltd but has no idea who the original Mr Nash might have been. Mike's grandfather started working at Billingsgate at the age of 13. He dropped out of school and did odd jobs around the market, usually cleaning up or sweeping the

floors. He worked hard for years and eventually got taken on by a merchant to sell fish. When the owner died, many years later, he left the stall to him and it was eventually passed down the generations to Mike. Recent expansion of the business has meant a longer working day for Mike and he'll often get by on just a couple of hours' sleep a night; sometimes none at all.

The other way to stake your claim to a Billingsgate stand is to buy an existing business or to take on a vacant stand. It can be difficult to infiltrate the close-knit market community but anyone not pulling their weight simply won't make a success of the stand. The natural ebb and flow of the market and tough working conditions mean it's the serious sellers who stay the distance. Brian took over his business 12 years ago and he still feels like a bit of a newcomer. Brothers Simon and Ben feel a bit more settled after 18 years on the market floor. They wanted to carry on the family fish trading tradition by setting up shop at Billingsgate. They used the name of their uncles' smoked salmon factory and have built up a great reputation and clientele for Bards Shellfish.

Life After Billingsgate

The porters certainly don't have a monopoly on extra curricular occupations. A number of merchants and their employees have chequered lives outside of the market hall, both previous and current. Terry used to play football for England and took time off work in 1960 to represent his country at the Olympic Games in Rome. His son carried on both the Billingsgate and football tradition by playing professionally for Chelsea before taking up his place in the market hall. Then there's Roger whose band 'Nights of Soul' toured all over Europe and released a number of CDs. Not content with being a rock star, Roger has also dabbled in stage hypnosis and has performed in Las Vegas. He's happy to

stick to his job at the market again for now, which is more than can be said for his son Dean who still manages to hold down two completely different careers. In the morning he works for J. Nash & Sons Ltd. Come the afternoon however, he heads straight to the gym where he reverts to his alter ego of the reigning British Masters Super Middleweight boxing champion. If he has a fight coming up he goes back to the gym for some sparring practise in the evening but tries to get enough sleep so he can be back at the market by 3am the next morning.

With such a varied cast of characters it's no surprise that Billingsgate is literally brimming over with vibrancy and personality. The merchants and porters carry on the history and traditions of Billingsgate and, although technology has come a long way and working conditions are much better than in years gone by, the market essentially operates in much the same way as it always has.

The natural ebb and flow of the market and tough working conditions mean it's the serious sellers who stay the distance

Salmon, Trout, Coarse Fish & related species

What's on Offer

Around 30 per cent of the fresh fish trade at Billingsgate market is farmed salmon. Up until 20 years ago it was a fraction of that, but with fish farming techniques constantly improving there is some excellent quality fish available and it's always very good value. High in omega 3 (approximately 1900 mg per 100 g, which is higher than herring and tuna) and hugely beneficial to long term health, we really can't eat enough of this type of fish.

The farmed Atlantic species on offer at the market are mainly from Scotland and Norway. Some merchants specialize in this fish and, depending on the time of year, they will have a selection on offer that is likely to include organic, RSPCA Freedom Food (also known as 'blue chip'), superior fish from a variety of sources, and fish coming in from specific lochs and producers that are highly regarded in the trade. Very small quantities of wild Atlantic fish from the Northeast of England and Scotland are available in season, which is short – and at a very premium price. Species of Pacific salmon are also available occasionally.

Salmon

Salmon can be purchased whole or gutted and as fillets and steaks. A popular course at the school is Every Which Way with Salmon as it demonstrates the versatility of this fish, not only in preparation but in cooking, too. A whole fish can be baked or poached and served hot or cold. The fish can be filleted or cut into sections (fillet, steaks and tail end – see page 37). To cook whole, cut out the gills with scissors and remove the scales (either with a professional scaler or the back of a knife). A whole side or fillet of salmon can be cooked as a single piece or cut into individual portions.

Salmon is suitable for every method of cooking, from deep-fried in tempura to poaching, grilling, pan-frying and roasting, and suits flavours as simple as herbs or a rich and buttery hollandaise to the complexity of teriyaki. To calculate the cooking time measure the thickest part of the fish with string. For every 2.5 cm (1 in) calculate 4 minutes cooking time. Brush the fish with oil and roast in an oven preheated to 220ºC/425ºF/Gas Mark 7.

FROM LEFT TO RIGHT: Salmon, carp and trout.

Trout

Closely related to salmon, there is always plenty of trout available on the market. Most of the trout sold is farmed rainbow trout, introduced into the UK from the USA at the end of the 19th century. It is a fish that has proven to be easy to farm, developing to a good marketable size in a fairly short space of time. Wild sea trout, also known as salmon trout, the migratory form of the brown trout, is readily available in season, and occasionally small quantities of farmed sea trout are sold. Brown trout, the indigenous species to the UK, is also organically farmed and is occasionally available at the market, and this makes an excellent choice.

Farmed trout is harvested to order and therefore can be very fresh when it comes to market, still in a state of rigor mortis. The fish has quite a generous coating of slime that needs to be rinsed away just prior to preparation to make is easier to handle. Rainbow trout is used in the school as an alternative to mackerel when we are demonstrating gutting, cleaning and filleting a round fish. It is a fish that works well with citrus flavours and aromatic herbs such as rosemary, tarragon and basil.

Coarse Fish

A variety of farmed freshwater species or coarse fish are sold at the market including pike, zander, sturgeon and carp. Although carp is by far the most extensively farmed species in the world, it is usually available only in small quantities on the market but is always popular with Chinese, Eastern Europeans and other Ethnic communities. For this reason there is increased availbility during holidays such as Christmas and Chinese New Year.

Many coarse fish have earned a reputation for having an earthy taste, due to feeding on food on the river bottom, often rooting about in mud to locate their prey. Nowadays these fish are often farmed on gravel, which helps improve the flavour.

Eel is sold live with the vast majority farmed in Holland and delivered to the market in specially adapted lorries fitted with freshwater tanks. Eel is also available ready cooked as jellied eel (a popular treat in many London areas) and smoked eel.

Potted Salmon

Serves 4 (as a starter)

225 g (8 oz) cooked salmon
50 g (2 oz) softened butter
1 tablespoon Worcestershire sauce
1 tablespoon anchovy essence
½ teaspoon cayenne pepper
salt and freshly ground black
   pepper
lemon juice, to taste
flat leaf parsley, to garnish

TO SERVE
4 rounds of wholemeal toast

This is an excellent way of using up leftover salmon and also works well with trout or carp.

Put the salmon, butter, Worcestershire sauce, anchovy essence and cayenne pepper into a food processor. Whiz together to form a smooth paste and season to taste with salt and pepper, adding lemon juice as required.

Spoon into 4 small dishes, garnish with parsley and serve with wholemeal toast.

Try this with any other leftover cooked fish, particularly trout

Poached Salmon with Samphire & Hollandaise

Serves 4

500 g (1¼ lb) salmon fillet,
   unskinned
2 litres (3½ pints) court bouillon
   (see page 130)
350 g (12 oz) samphire
hollandaise sauce
   (see page 148)
grated zest and juice of 2 limes

Preheat the oven to 190°C/375°F/gas mark 5. Pin-bone the salmon fillet and cut into 4 equal portions.

Put the fish in a large roasting tin, skin side up, and pour over the court bouillon. Bake in the oven for 15–18 minutes or until the fish is opaque. Remove from the oven and leave in the liquid for a few minutes while you prepare the remainder of the dish.

Meanwhile, blanch the samphire in boiling water for 1–2 minutes, drain and refresh under cold running water for a few seconds. Drain and arrange on 4 warm serving plates.

Season the hollandaise sauce with the grated lime zest and enough juice to make the sauce quite tangy. Arrange the salmon on the samphire and spoon the sauce over the top just before serving.

Teriyaki
Salmon

Serves 4

4 salmon fillets (tail end pieces),
    each about 150 g (5 oz)
1 tablespoon oil
2 spring onions, finely sliced
1 tablespoon sesame seeds

FOR THE TERIYAKI MARINADE
4 tablespoons dark soy sauce
1 tablespoon grated fresh root
    ginger
2 tablespoons mirin
2 tablespoons rice wine vinegar
½ teaspoon wasabi paste

We run a couple of Japanese and sushi/sashimi courses at the school and this recipe is included in the course introduction. Teriyaki, literally meaning 'shine grill', is either fish or chicken marinated in soy, and mirin (sweet rice wine) gives the fish a lovely sticky glaze.

Put the salmon into a shallow dish. Mix together the ingredients for the marinade and pour over the fish, turning the fillets so they are evenly coated. Cover and leave in the refrigerator for 4 hours.

Lift the fish from the marinade, reserving the marinade. Heat the oil in a large, nonstick frying pan, add the fish and pan-fry for 2–3 minutes on each side. Transfer the cooked fish to a plate.

Add the spring onions and sesame seeds to the frying pan and toss over the heat for 1–2 minutes or until the seeds are lightly browned. Replace the fish and add the remaining marinade, bring to the boil and simmer for a few seconds until sticky. Serve immediately.

"At home I grill salmon fillets (at Nash we sell them already pin-boned) and serve them with sun-dried tomatoes and a dollop of marmalade – superb." **Bill, James Nash & Sons**

Roast
Salmon Fillet
with Ginger & Chilli Dressing

Serves 4

**750 g (1¾ lb) salmon fillet,
   unskinned and pin-boned**

FOR THE DRESSING
2 tablespoons rice wine vinegar
grated zest and juice of 2 limes
4 tablespoons extra virgin olive oil
1 tablespoon sesame oil
2 tablespoons light soy sauce
2 tablespoons grated root ginger
1 teaspoon honey
**2 seeded and finely chopped
   red chillies**
handful of chopped coriander
**salt and freshly ground black
   pepper**

TO SERVE
rice or noodles

Preheat the oven to 200°C/400°F/gas mark 6.

Put the salmon on a large baking sheet, skin side down, and bake for 15–18 minutes or until the fish is opaque and will flake if gently pressed.

Meanwhile, mix together the ingredients for the dressing and season to taste with salt and pepper.

Remove the cooked fish from the oven, transfer to a serving dish and spoon over the dressing. Serve with rice or noodles.

Try this with trout or sea bass

"My wife cooks a lovely bit of salmon. She wraps it in foil before baking in the oven and serves it with potatoes and peas." **Terry, J.J. Ovenell**

Court
Bouillon

1 tablespoon olive oil
2 large onions, finely sliced
1 large carrot, peeled and finely
    sliced
1 celery stick, finely sliced
150 ml (5 fl oz) white wine
1.5 litres (2½ pints) water
1 teaspoon black peppercorns
1 bay leaf
1 sprig of thyme
a few parsley stalks
pinch of salt
splash of white wine vinegar

This classic fish poaching liquid is a lightly acidulated vegetable stock. After it has been used for cooking seafood it can be re-used as a base for soups or sauces. This recipe is perfect for boiling all types of seafood.

Heat the oil in a large saucepan. Add the onions, carrot and celery and stir over a low to medium heat until beginning to soften. Add the remaining ingredients, bring to the boil and simmer over a low heat for 20 minutes. Cool, strain and use as required.

"I like all fish – steamed, fried or anyway it comes. A whole fish baked in the oven with a bit of garlic and served with rice and salad is just beautiful." Tom, A. A. Lyons

Ginger-cured
Salmon

Serves 4

450 g (1 lb) salmon fillet, skinned

FOR THE CURE
1 tablespoon wasabi paste
2 red chillies, seeded and finely
    chopped
1 green chilli, seeded and finely
    chopped
1 teaspoon ground coriander
50 g (2 oz) fine sea salt
1 tablespoon crushed peppercorns
5 tablespoons rice wine vinegar
3 tablespoons grated root ginger

TO SERVE
150 ml (5 fl oz) fromage frais
2 tablespoons chopped coriander

Gravadlax (meaning 'buried salmon' from the traditional method of curing the fish in the ground) is a Scandinavian speciality, but there are many flavours that work well as a marinade. This has a Pacific rim twist.

Pin-bone the salmon fillet if necessary.

Mix together the ingredients for the cure. Put half of the cure on a piece of clingfilm, place the salmon on top and press the remaining cure on top. Wrap well in clingfilm, place in a dish and weigh down with a couple of plates. Leave in the refrigerator for 24–36 hours.

Scrape off and discard the excess mixture from the salmon, then slice the fish very thinly, using a smoked salmon knife or very sharp carving knife.

Arrange the slices on a serving dish and serve with fromage frais and chopped coriander.

Seafood
Lasagne

Serves 8

400 g (14 oz) salmon fillet, skinned and pin-boned
200 g (7 oz) coley fillet, skinned and pin-boned
salt and freshly ground black pepper
1 whole egg, separated
75 g (3 oz) butter
150 g (5 oz) cherry tomatoes, halved
1 clove garlic, crushed
75 g (3 oz) plain flour
600 ml (1 pint) milk
200 ml (7 fl oz) crème fraîche
2 tablespoons chopped basil
2 tablespoons chopped chives
2 tablespoons chopped parsley
450 g (1 lb) cooked North Atlantic prawns, peeled
150 g (5 oz) cooked cockles
8 sheets fresh lasagne verde
100 g (4 oz) mozzarella cheese, grated
3 tablespoons freshly grated Parmesan cheese

Preheat the oven to 190°C/375°F/gas mark 5. Cut the salmon and coley into 5 cm (2 in) pieces and mix in a bowl. Season with salt and pepper and add the egg white only. Set aside.

Melt the butter in a large saucepan, add the tomatoes and garlic and cook over a low heat for 2–3 minutes. Stir in the flour and gradually blend in the milk. Bring to the boil and simmer for 2–3 minutes. Stir in 2 tablespoons of the crème fraîche and the herbs and season to taste with salt and pepper.

Mix the salmon and coley into the sauce together with the prawns and cockles.

Put a couple of sheets of lasagne in the bottom of an ovenproof dish and spoon some of the fish mixture on top. Cover with further sheets of lasagne and continue to layer, finishing with a layer of pasta. Mix the remaining crème fraîche with the egg yolk and cheeses and spoon over the top sheets of lasagne.

Bake in the oven for 30–35 minutes or until the fish is cooked and the sauce is bubbling. Serve immediately.

Carp Schnitzel
with Salsa Verde   Serves 4

1 carp, about 1.5 kg (3¼ lb), filleted
   (see page 38)
1 egg, beaten
3 tablespoons polenta
2 tablespoons flour
2 teaspoons paprika (hot or sweet)
salt and freshly ground black
   pepper
5 tablespoons olive oil

FOR THE SALSA VERDE
4 tablespoons chopped flat leaf
   parsley
1 tablespoon chopped chives
1 tablespoon chopped tarragon
1 tablespoon chopped dill
1 clove garlic, crushed
2 teaspoons anchovy essence
4 tablespoons fresh breadcrumbs
5 tablespoons extra virgin olive oil
lemon juice, to taste

TO SERVE
new potatoes

Pin-bone the carp fillets (see page 35) but leave the skin on. Cut through the fillets at close intervals, pushing the knife just through the skin to open the flesh, and cut each fillet into 4 small portions. Brush the carp with the beaten egg.

In a bowl mix together the polenta, flour and paprika and season with salt and pepper. Roll the fillets in this mixture, making sure that each piece is well coated.

Heat the oil in a large frying pan, add the fillets and fry over a low to medium heat for 2–3 minutes on each side. Transfer to a serving plate and keep warm.

Meanwhile, make the salsa. Put the herbs, garlic, anchovy essence and breadcrumbs into a food processor. Whiz together until well chopped and add the oil. Continue to process until well emulsified, season to taste with salt and pepper and add lemon juice as required.

Drizzle the salsa over the fish and serve with new potatoes.

Try this with pike, zander or trout fillets

Carp
Frame Soup

Serves 4

FOR THE STOCK
1 tablespoon olive oil
1 onion, roughly chopped
1 clove garlic, chopped
1 celery stick, sliced
leek trimmings (from soup)
4 teaspoons tomato purée
1 carp fish frame (leftover from
   filleting)
1 litre (1¾ pints) water
1 bay leaf
sprigs of thyme

FOR THE SOUP
25 g (1 oz) butter
1 small leek, sliced
2 teaspoons paprika
1 large potato, about 250 g (9 oz),
   peeled and diced
salt and freshly ground black
   pepper

Make the stock. Heat the oil in a large saucepan, add the vegetables and stir over a medium heat for 5–7 minutes or until beginning to soften. Add the tomato purée and carp frame and cook for a further 2 minutes. Pour over the water and add the herbs. Bring to the boil, skim off any scum that rises to the surface and cook, uncovered, over a low heat for 25 minutes. Strain and reserve the liquid, discarding the frame and vegetables.

Make the soup. Melt the butter in a clean saucepan, add the leek and paprika and cook, stirring occasionally, over a low heat for 4–5 minutes or until the leek has begun to soften. Stir in the potato, cook for a further minute and add the reserved stock. Bring to the boil and season generously with salt and pepper. Cook for 5–7 minutes or until the potatoes are cooked, adjust the seasoning and serve.

"I never ate fish when I was a kid but I'm a boxer when I'm not at the market so now it's a big part of my diet. It's good for training." **Deano, James Nash & Sons**

Baked Trout

Serves 2

with Crème Fraîche & Caper Berries

2 small trout, scaled, gutted and gills removed
salt and freshly ground black pepper

FOR THE SAUCE
15 g (½ oz) butter
2 shallots, finely chopped
1 clove garlic, crushed
5 tablespoons dry white wine
1 tablespoon white wine vinegar
150 ml (5 fl oz) half-fat crème fraîche
1 tablespoon chopped dill
1 tablespoon chopped chives
12 caper berries, stalks removed and halved

Preheat the oven to 190°C/375°F/gas mark 5.

Put the trout in a large, foil-lined roasting tin and season lightly with salt and pepper. Bake the fish in the oven for 15–18 minutes or until the eye of the fish has turned white and the flesh feels flaky underneath the skin.

Meanwhile, make the sauce. Melt the butter in a small saucepan, add the shallots and garlic and cook over a low heat for 2–3 minutes or until beginning to soften. Add the white wine and vinegar, bring to the boil and simmer until it has reduced to about 3 tablespoons. Stir the crème fraîche into the reduction, bring to the boil and add the herbs and caper berries. Season the sauce to taste.

Pull away the skin from each trout and transfer to a serving dish. Spoon the sauce over the fish and serve.

Try this with salmon or red mullet

Shellfish at Billingsgate

Billingsgate is not only the largest inland fish market in the UK, but also the largest shellfish market and there is always a wonderful selection of shellfish on offer. On the whole shellfish from the UK are some of the most sustainable seafood available and also some of the safest to enjoy. Although most of these species are in plentiful supply there are some issues surrounding the harvesting of some species using dredges. For up-to-date information The Shellfish Association of Great Britain give greater detail at www.shellfish.org.

We tend to find that many people coming to the market for the first time don't know what to choose and feel apprehensive about what to buy and how to check that it is safe to eat. People are often under the impression that shellfish are not a healthy choice to eat, but quite the opposite is true. The Shellfish Association of Great Britain has published a small pamphlet explaining how many misconceptions about shellfish are untrue, and this can be obtained via their website.

There are many rigorous regulations in place when it comes to the growing, harvesting, preparing for sale and the selling of shellfish. Anyone buying from the wide selection at Billingsgate can purchase safe in the knowledge that it is good to eat and will be of the highest possibly quality. And it goes without saying that it will be excellent value for money! Any merchant selling shellfish will be able to give you lots of information about where the seafood has come from, how it was collected, when it was harvested, how to store it and how to cook it.

The school has collaborated with The Shellfish Association of Great Britain on short films extolling the virtues of shellfish. The aim of each film is to demonstrate how shellfish can be prepared from scratch in a matter of minutes and to demystify and promote a much under valued food. The films can be viewed at www.youtube.com/user/ShellfishGB. The school works with a wide selection of shellfish and enjoys promoting the great health benefits of enjoying these as much as fish!

Oysters, Whelks, Winkles, Abalone, Scallops, Clams, Cockles & Mussels

Oysters

What's on Offer

Pacific or 'Rock' oysters are available year round; these are farmed and are harvested in many areas but most of the oysters sold at Billingsgate come from the clean waters around the British Isles and France and are very sustainable. Native or 'Flat' oysters are more expensive and are only available from September to the end of April, eaten when there is an 'R' in the month. Oysters are unique in that the flavour and texture of both types can vary depending on the time of year and in which water they are grown. Oysters can be bought by the box or loose by the dozen or half dozen.

Storage and Preparation

The merchants will know where the oysters they are selling were harvested and on what day. Oysters can keep in good condition for several days. To store, place the oysters cupped side down (this prevents loss of juice) on a plate, loosely cover and keep refrigerated. Before you attempt to open an oyster check that the shells are tightly closed. If a shell is open at all and doesn't close on tapping, it MUST be discarded as it may not be safe to eat.

To open (shuck) an oyster you will need an oyster knife. Hold the oyster very firmly in a thick cloth to protect your hands, insert the blade of the knife at the hinge end and twist until the tip is lodged very firmly and is unlikely to slip. Release some pressure and then gently lever up the knife. Work the knife from left to right and the shell should open. Remove the top shell and discard. Release the oyster from the bottom shell by running a knife underneath.

One of the benefits of including oysters in your diet is that they have good mineral content. Many people are surprised to discover that half a dozen oysters provide the same omega 3 levels as a fillet of mackerel and they are known to concentrate zinc in the diet, so a very good excuse to tuck in and enjoy!

Whelks and Winkles

What's on Offer

These two species of shellfish are available at the market live, cooked in the shell and cooked and brined. These can be purchased by the scoop (most merchants prefer to sell them in 500 g/1¼ lb increments), and when cooked they are sold in 1–2 kg (2–4½ lb) 'vac-pac' bags. They are classified as gastropods (univalves) and they are snail-like in appearance.

Storage and Preparation

If purchased live you will need to check for signs of life before cooking. The operculum (horny foot) closing the shell should be tightly shut. Discard any that have a hollow ring when tapped or that smell of amonia. Simply boil them in lightly salted water – whelks take between 5 and 7 minutes and winkles (Periwinkles officially) take 3–4 minutes depending on size.

**CLOCKWISE FROM TOP LEFT: Winkles (in bowl), rope grown mussels, whelks (in bowl), Venus clams, native oysters, razor clams, palourde clams (in bowl), American hard shell clam, diver caught scallop, cockles.
IN THE MIDDLE: Amande clams, Pacific/rock oysters.**

To serve simply brush with oil and serve with a bowl of vinegar and a slice of chilli or some lemon – if you like shellfish these are a real treat (a small fork or in the case of winkles, a pin is required to remove the meat from the shell).

Abalone

This shellfish comes in a single shell and are sold individually. They are very occasionally available for sale from certain areas in the Channel islands, imported from South Africa, New Zealand or farmed in France. They are very expensive, even on the market and they are a niche product. They have a unique texture and flavour and steaming or flash frying in garlic butter are both popular methods for cooking them.

Scallops

What's on Offer
Scallops can be purchased live in the shell or ready prepared in boxes of 1–2 kg (2–4½ lb) weight. They are also available prepared (on and off the shell) and frozen. The cost can vary depending on what you choose. If you want to prepare your own, some merchants will sell 'Divers' (diver harvested scallops), which are usually large and pristine in appearance and, although quite costly, are well worth the money. Dredged scallops are less expensive and can be a little muddy and the shells can be chipped. Ready prepared scallops may be labelled as 'dry' meaning that there is no added water (these are more expensive) – others will have a little liquid in the box. Queen scallops are a smaller species and are sold prepared on the half shell or completely prepared removed from the shell. Availability can vary depending on weather conditions and the time of year. Most merchants will sell these by the half or full dozen.

Storage and Preparation
If you buy scallops in the shell it is a good idea to prepare them by removing the meat from the shells as soon as you can and then refrigerate the meats until you need them. There are various ways of preparing a scallop. A fishmonger will prepare it so that it is trimmed and then left attached to the flat shell. For preparation at home use a blunt knife or oyster knife to lever the shell open at the hinge. Run the knife along the inside of the rounded shell to release the scallop and remove. Lift the scallop from the flat shell by running a knife under the white meat, close to the shell. The scallop then needs to be cleaned. Remove the black sac (stomach), the frill and trim so that all is left is the coral (orange and cream coloured roe) and the white muscle meat. Wash if necessary and pat dry.

Clams and Cockles

What's on Offer
There is a great selection of clams on offer including palourdes, Venus (surf clams), amande and American hard-shell (cherry stone clams) that can be steamed open and the meat used for chowders, soups and for stuffing. Razor clams and gooey ducks (or sand gropers, pidducks or 'Piss clams' in the US) are also available. Some merchants sell clams loose allowing the purchaser to choose the weight, others will sell them by the box. These clams are harvested from various areas, either farmed or wild. The merchants who sell these have all the knowledge – so if you are interested to learn more, speak with them.

A majority of cockles for sale on the market are freshly cooked, cooked and frozen or freshly cooked and brined (wonderful!) and very small quantities are sold live. They are a great treat and are a popular purchase for many. Live cockles come in a variety of colours – we often see those from Scotland in taupe coloured shells, whereas those landed on the Dorset coast have a marbled shell which is not dissimilar to a palourde. Most merchants will sell these by the scoop or in pre-measured bags of 500 g (1¼ lb) plus.

Storage and Preparation
Like all bivalves cockles and clams can survive for several days if stored correctly. Keep them refrigerated in a bowl covered with a damp cloth. DO NOT soak them in water and ALWAYS prepare them carefully. Just before cooking check that they are still alive (the shells should be tightly shut). If the shell is open give it a sharp tap and if the shell doesn't fully close, discard it. Throw away any that are damaged, cracked or broken and wash them carefully before cooking.

Mussels

The autumn, winter and early spring months are a good time of year for enjoying mussels. They are always excellent value for money and are usually available in 2 kg (4½ lb) or 5 kg (11 lb) bags at the market. As many mussels are now farmed they are available all year, although during the summer months you can't guarantee what the quality will be like. The merchants sell them year round and many chefs purchase them as they are an excellent addition to fish stock.

What's on Offer
Both wild (dredged) and rope-grown mussels are sold. You can identify wild mussels by the black shell, which is scuffed in appearance. Rope-grown (farmed mussels) have black glossy shells and have fewer barnacles and therefore generally require less preparation. Rope-grown have slightly thinner shells so they take a little less time to cook, too, and are really the ultimate in sustainable seafood (often referred to as the most sustainable form of omega 3) so can be enjoyed completely guilt free!

Storage and Preparation
They can survive for several days if stored correctly. Keep them refrigerated in a bowl covered with a damp cloth. DO NOT soak them in water and ALWAYS prepare them carefully. Prepare them when you are just about to cook them. Check that they are still alive (the shells should be closed). If the shell is open give it a sharp tap, if the shell doesn't close, discard. Check each mussel for damage and discard those that are cracked or broken. The mussels will then need washing and 'debearding'. The beard or byssus thread is protein that the mussel 'spins' to help attach itself to the rope or rock on which it is growing, it looks like a strand of seaweed and should be pulled away. Scrape away any barnacles with a knife. It is also important to note that any mussel that has NOT opened during cooking should be discarded, too.

Sea Urchins

These are available in small quantities during spring and autumn months. In a black/brown prickly shell they are simply opened on the underside and enjoyed scooped directly from the shell.

Oysters
in the Half Shell

12 oysters, native or rocks
   (see page 142)
crushed ice

RED WINE AND SHALLOT DRESSING
2 shallots, finely chopped
5 tablespoons red wine vinegar

BLOODY MARY DRESSING
1 teaspoon tomato purée
1 teaspoon creamed horseradish
1 tablespoon vodka

SOY AND SESAME DRESSING
2 tablespoons dark soy sauce
sprinkling of sesame oil
1 spring onion, finely sliced
splash of sesame oil

**TRUFFLE OIL AND TARRAGON
   DRESSING**
juice and zest of 1 lemon
1 tablespoon chopped fresh
   tarragon
splash of truffle oil

Our Every Which Way courses at the school give our guests the opportunity to work with a variety of species. They learn how to prepare the seafood and also discover various methods of cooking. Our Every Which Way with Oysters course is popular and in addition to the traditional accompaniments of Tabasco sauce and lemon wedges, we encourage our visitors to experiment and try new flavour combinations, such as those used here. The soy and sesame dressing was discovered quite by accident as this isn't a combination that would usually spring to mind, but it complements the oysters perfectly.

To serve, shuck the oysters and remove the top shells. Release from the bottom shell, then arrange on some crushed ice and garnish with lemon. Mix together the dressing of your choice. Traditional accompaniments are always lemon wedges and Tabasco sauce. Serve these alongside the oysters.

Oysters
Rockefeller

2 dozen oysters, shucked
145 g (5 oz) watercress, washed,
  blanched and chopped
hollandaise sauce (see below)
1 teaspoon anchovy essence
  (or to taste)
1 teaspoon Worcestershire sauce
  (or to taste)
cayenne pepper

Preheat the grill to its highest setting.

Lift the oysters from their shells. Place a spoonful of watercress on each shell and replace the oyster. Season the hollandaise sauce with anchovy essence, Worcestershire sauce and cayenne pepper. Spoon 1 teaspoon over each oyster. Arrange on a baking sheet.

Grill the oysters for 1 minute or until the sauce has browned lightly.

Remove the oysters from the grill and sprinkle with a little more cayenne pepper. Serve immediately.

Hollandaise Sauce

6 tablespoons wine vinegar
6 black peppercorns
1 bay leaf
1 blade of mace
4 egg yolks
salt
200 g (7 oz) unsalted butter
lemon juice

Put the vinegar, peppercorns, bay leaf and mace in a small, heavy saucepan and simmer until reduced to 2 tablespoons.

Put the egg yolks and salt into a blender and process lightly. Add the hot vinegar reduction and whiz together.

Heat the butter until it is hot and foaming. With the blender machine running, pour the hot butter over the egg yolks in a slow, steady stream. If the mixture looks as if it will curdle (separate) add a splash of very cold water or a small squeeze of lemon juice. Serve warm.

Winkle & Watercress

Sandwiches

Makes 2 rounds of sandwiches

250 g (9 oz) cooked winkles
salt and freshly ground black
   pepper
splash of non-brewed vinegar
4 slices brown or white bread
butter
large handful of watercress

This recipe was given to us by Ken Condon, a retired fishmonger who works with us at the school and who bought from the market for many years for his well-known fish shop in Stockwell, south London. This is one of his favourite tea-time treats. He likes to use Vinney's non-brewed vinegar, which he buys from Billingsgate Market.

Tease the winkles from their shells with a pin and remove the operculum (the hard core at one end). Season with salt, pepper and vinegar.

Butter the bread and pack with watercress and winkles. Cut and serve.

Scallops
with Chorizo

Serves 2

50 g (2 oz) chorizo, thickly sliced
6 prepared scallops
1 red pepper, seeded and finely
    sliced
3 spring onions, finely sliced
1 tablespoon chopped parsley
squeeze of lemon juice
salt and freshly ground black
    pepper

Heat the chorizo in a frying pan and cook over a medium heat until the fat begins to run. Increase the heat and cook until beginning to frazzle. Transfer the chorizo on to a plate and set aside.

Heat the frying pan until the fat is just beginning to smoke. Add the scallops and pan-fry over a high heat for 1–2 minutes on each side or until the scallops are lightly seared.

Replace the chorizo, add the red pepper and spring onions and toss over a low heat for 2–3 minutes. Stir in the parsley and seasoning. Squeeze over lemon juice and serve immediately.

"A favourite market breakfast is scallops with bacon and fried tomatoes served with white bread and butter. None of that fancy stuff, just good simple food."

Don & Tony, J. Bennett Jnr.

Scallop

Ceviche

Serves 2 (as a starter)

4 scallops (white meat only)
finely grated zest and juice of 1 lime
½ red chilli, seeded and finely
   chopped
splash of extra virgin olive oil
2 teaspoons honey
1 red or yellow pepper, seeded and
   finely diced
1 tablespoon finely chopped dill or
   flat leaf parsley
freshly ground black pepper

Ceviche originates from South America and is traditionally served as a started or appetiser. The citrus marinate works well with white fish as well as shellfish.

Finely dice the scallop meat and arrange on a flat plate. Sprinkle over the lime zest and juice and chilli. Cover and refrigerate for 30 minutes or until the scallops begin to turn opaque.

Drizzle with a little oil and honey, and sprinkle with the pepper and dill or parsley. Season with pepper and serve.

Try this with monkfish

Roast Scallops

with Leek & Ginger

Serves 2 (as a starter)

4 scallops in their shells
about 450 g (1 lb) ready-made
 puff pastry
1 small leek, finely shredded
1 small piece root ginger, peeled
 and finely shredded
½ teaspoon sesame oil
large splash of dark soy sauce
salt and freshly ground black
 pepper

Open the scallops with a strong knife and prepare. Remove and reserve the roes and cut the white meat in half horizontally. Discard the frills and black stomach sacs. Scrub the scallop shells (tops and bottoms) under running cold water and set aside. Blanch the scallops in boiling water for 2 minutes, refresh with cold water and set aside.

Roll out the pastry and cut it into strips long enough to run around the lip of the shells. Preheat the oven to 220°C/425°F/gas mark 7.

Put some leek and ginger in the scallop shells. Put the roe and 3 rounds of white meat in each shell and drizzle with sesame oil and soy sauce. Season with salt and pepper.

Put the empty shells on top of the filled shells and edge each with a strip of pastry brushed with the water to seal completely. Bake in the oven for 10–12 minutes, according to the size of the scallops, and serve, still piping hot, in the shells.

Try this with raw prawns

Grilled
Razor Clams

Serves 4

with Garlic Butter

20 razor clams
50 g (2 oz) butter
2 cloves garlic, chopped
1 tablespoon chopped parsley
squeeze of lemon juice
salt and freshly ground black
  pepper

TO GARNISH
flat leaf parsley
lemon wedges

Preheat the grill to its highest setting.

Check the clams are alive – the shells should shut tightly when tapped. Arrange the clams on a baking sheet and grill for 1 minute or until the clams begin to open.

Meanwhile, melt the butter in a small saucepan. Add the garlic, parsley and lemon juice and season to taste. Remove the clams from the grill and brush with some of the garlic butter. Return to the grill and cook for 1–2 further minutes until the clams are fully opened.

Transfer the clams on to a serving dish, season with salt and pepper and garnish with parsley and lemon wedges. Serve hot or warm.

Try this with surf clams

Seared Scallop & Bacon Omelette

Serves 4

4 rashers of streaky bacon, diced

4 large scallops, cut in half horizontally

5 large eggs, beaten

2 tablespoons milk

1 tablespoon chopped chives

salt and freshly ground black pepper

Freshly shucked king scallops, simply pan-fried with bacon, are a popular breakfast with the fisheries inspectors at the market. This omelette is also a great start to the day.

Cook the bacon in a large, nonstick frying pan (measuring approximately 20 cm/8 in) until crispy and remove with a slotted spoon, leaving as much fat in the pan as possible.

Heat the bacon fat until very hot, add the scallops and sear quickly on both sides for 1 minute.

Meanwhile, whisk together the eggs, milk, chives and salt and pepper.

Return the bacon to the pan and pour over the omelette mixture. Stir carefully and cook over a low heat for 2–3 minutes or until the omelette is just set. Slide on to plates to serve.

Steamed
Cockles

Serves 6 (as a starter)

with Greek Yogurt & Capers

1 kg (2¼ lb) cockles, cleaned
150 ml (5 fl oz) water

FOR THE DRESSING
5 tablespoons Greek yogurt
2 tablespoons capers
1 tablespoon chopped dill
1 tablespoon chopped parsley
grated zest and juice of ½ lime
salt and freshly ground black
** pepper**

Wash the cockles and check that all the shells are closed and that none are damaged. Cook in a saucepan with the water for a few minutes until opened. Lift the cockles from the cooking liquid and remove from the shells.

Make the dressing. Mix together the yogurt, capers, chopped herbs and lime zest and juice and season to taste. Toss the cockles in the dressing or serve separately, with the dressing as a dip.

Try this with palourde or venus clams

Coconut & Chilli Steamed
Palourdes

Serves 4 (as a starter)

1 kg (2¼ lb) palourde clams
2 red chillies, seeded and chopped
1 clove garlic, crushed
1 lemon grass stalk, thickly sliced
1 teaspoon grated fresh root ginger
200 ml (7 fl oz) coconut milk
handful of chopped coriander
   leaves

Wash the clams and check that they are all tightly shut. Discard any that are damaged or do not close when tapped sharply.

Put the chillies, garlic, lemon grass, ginger and coconut milk into a large saucepan. Bring to the boil and simmer for 1 minute.

Add the prepared clams, cover with a tight-fitting lid and cook for 4–5 minutes or until the clams are fully opened. Lift the clams into a serving dish, discarding any that are not open.

Bring the cooking liquid to the boil and simmer for 1 minute. Stir in the coriander and spoon over the clams to serve.

Try this with mussels and razor or surf clams

Clams
with Spaghetti

Serves 4

1 kg (2¼ lb) small Venus clams in
   their shells
5 tablespoons extra virgin olive oil
5 tablespoons wine
5 tablespoons water
2–3 cloves garlic, finely sliced
24 cherry tomatoes, halved
salt and freshly ground black
   pepper
2 tablespoons chopped basil
450 g (15 oz) fresh spaghetti

This is our take on Spaghetti con Vongole. The clams used in this classic Venetian dish would be the little clams that come from the Adriatic Sea.

Wash and scrub the clams thoroughly under cold running water. Discard any that are damaged or do not close when tapped.

Heat 1 tablespoon oil in a large saucepan, add the clams, wine and water, cover and shake until the clams have opened. Discard any that are still closed. Remove and reserve the clams.

Heat the remaining oil in a clean saucepan, add the garlic and cook for 1 minute to soften. Add the tomatoes and toss over a high heat for 1–2 minutes or until the tomatoes begin to soften. Season lightly and stir in the basil.

Cook the spaghetti in plenty of boiling salted water. When al dente, drain and mix with the tomato mixture and toss in the clams. Serve immediately.

Mussel
Chowder

Serves 2

1 kg (2¼ lb) rope-grown mussels,
　scrubbed and debearded
1 clove garlic
150 ml (5 fl oz) white wine
2 leeks, finely sliced
25 g (1 oz) butter
large pinch of saffron
4 medium potatoes, about 300 g
　(11 oz) in total, diced
2 tablespoons plain flour
300 ml (10 fl oz) milk
1 tablespoon chopped thyme
salt and freshly ground black
　pepper

TO SERVE
crusty bread

Prepare the mussels, checking each for damage and signs of life. Discard any that are cracked or broken and those that do not shut when sharply tapped.

Put the mussels in a large saucepan with the garlic and wine. Cover and steam for 4–5 minutes or until the mussels are fully open. Lift the mussels into a separate bowl, discarding any that have not opened, and reserve the cooking liquid. Remove the mussel meat from the shells and set aside.

Cook the leeks in the butter until softened but not brown, add the saffron and potatoes and fry for a further 4–5 minutes. Add the flour and cook for 1 minute, then carefully blend in the milk. Whisk in the strained mussel liquor and bring to the boil. Simmer until the potatoes are cooked and the soup has a good flavour. Stir in the thyme and mussels, heat until piping hot and season to taste. Serve in deep bowls with crusty bread.

"I like mussels with a jar of red chilli sauce. None of this white wine stuff, just a nice jar of chilli sauce and you're away." **Simon, Bards Shellfish**

Garlic & Parsley
Mussel Parcels

Serves 2

1 kg (2¼ lb) prepared mussels
1 clove garlic, chopped
2 tablespoons chopped parsley
squeeze of lemon juice
freshly ground black pepper
25 g (1 oz) butter

TO SERVE
warm bread

This dish can be served as a light lunch or supper and is ideal for a quick and informal meal.

Preheat the oven to 220°C/425°F/gas mark 7. Preheat a baking sheet. Cut 2 heart shapes from pieces of good-quality greaseproof paper about 60 cm (24 in) long. Fold each in half to crease the centre line.

Put half the mussels on one piece of greaseproof paper. Sprinkle over half of the garlic, parsley and lemon juice and season with pepper only. Dot the top with the butter. Repeat with the remaining ingredients.

Fold over the greaseproof paper and twist the edges together to form a secure parcel that still allows steam to circulate. Place on the hot baking sheet and bake in the oven for 4–5 minutes. Each guest will open their own parcel; advise them to discard any mussels that have not opened. Serve with plenty of warm bread.

Fish
Traditions

Britain always used to be regarded as a fish-eating nation. Traditionally, fish and shellfish have played an important role in British society and its culinary history. It goes without saying that an island with a coastline stretching for about 5,000 miles should be pretty good at catching and eating fish. However, our eating habits, incomes, traditions and tastes have all changed – people move around more nowadays and the fishing industry has gone into decline in many areas. All this has meant that a number of our fish traditions have slipped away or disappeared completely. While many people still consider our national dish to be fish and chips, it's competing for its place on the dinner table with many other foods. The traditions that saw fish firmly entrenched on the weekly menu have largely been lost or forgotten and it's time to start celebrating this nutritious, versatile and economical ingredient once again.

Fish and Chips

When asked to conjure up images of Britain, fish and chips eaten out of newspaper on a windswept beach would surely be somewhere towards the top of the list. Of course, nowadays health and safety regulations stipulate that fish and chips can't be served in newspaper and people tend to take them home to eat them, but they're still as British as football and queuing. Although the number of fish and chip shops has declined markedly since their heyday in the 1930s, this simple meal is still our most popular takeaway dish by far and the fryers aren't going to be switched off any time soon. There is hot dispute over whether the first chippie was opened in London or Lancashire and it's probably a claim that will be contested ad finitum.

Regardless of where that first cod fillet was dipped in batter and lowered into bubbling fat, the popularity of fish and chips quickly spread and it was informally adopted as a national dish. This warm parcel of fish and potatoes was so highly regarded and unanimously consumed by the general public, that it was one of the only foods not to be rationed during the Second World War.

The First Fishmongers

Fishmongers have sold their wares to the public for hundreds of years. In Victorian times, much of their trade came from the poorer areas, as fish and shellfish were cheap and plentiful and provided some much needed protein in a mundane diet. Vendors would push their carts or barrows around the streets of working class areas and a good pitch could prove to be lucrative. They could often be found just outside a public house, waiting for hungry patrons to emerge and buy a snack or something for tea on their way home. It wasn't until much later on that the likes of mussels and oysters moved up the social ladder, as the wealthier classes got a taste for them and they began to be viewed as a luxury foodstuff. Traditional fishmongers' shops used to be a regular feature on many high streets but, as with so many independent retailers, many succumbed to the efficient and all-encompassing shopping experience of the supermarket. Many businesses simply couldn't compete and were forced to close their shutters and cease trading. However, as people have become more aware of the environment and sustainability issues, the traditional fishmonger is once again returning to our towns and villages. Many people are reverting to the shopping habits of previous generations and independent traders are enjoying a comeback.

Fish on a Friday

Fish has found its way into many traditions and observances over the centuries and religion has had a significant part to play. A number of religions include periods of fasting or abstinence, which is seen as a form of discipline. In Christianity, and the Catholic Church in particular, removing meat from the menu on a Friday was a widespread form of abstinence. This meant that fish was traditionally eaten on a Friday night and, although the custom still remains, it is not commonly adhered to. Regardless of religion, fish on a Friday would be a great way to ensure everyone had at least one serving of fish per week.

Jellied Eels

Jellied eels are so entrenched in East End folklore that the two have become pretty much intertwined. Eels were a staple food for the poor in the Victorian era, as they were so plentiful, but their less than enticing appearance and the cold, gelatinous flavour made them something of an acquired taste for those who weren't brought up on them. A trip to the pie and mash shop would be a weekly treat for many East End families and jellied eels would often be the meal of choice.

Shellfish for Sunday Tea

This is another traditional custom that hasn't stood the test of time and many people have never tasted the vast array of wonderfully fresh shellfish that's available from British shores. In the past, families would gather together for tea on a Sunday. As people tended to live closer together a couple of generations ago, this might mean no more than popping down the road or across town. Everyone would take some food to the hosts' house and then they'd all sit down together and eat. The food often included shellfish – shrimps, cockles, whelks – and maybe some bread and cakes. It was a chance for families to relax, enjoy a meal and spend some quality time together after a hard week at work.

"You can't beat fish & chips. When I was a kid we had fish & chips from the chippie every Friday. Everyone did." **Colin, porter**

Crab, Lobster, Langoustine & Prawns

What's on Offer

There is a wide selection of shellfish from this group available at the market and they generally offer great value for money. Always ask the merchant you are purchasing from if you would like to know where the product has come from or for preparation tips.

Prawns

There are plenty of prawns on the market, some sold in boxes packed in ice and some frozen. Ninety nine per cent of all prawns on the market, whether they are cooked or raw, will have been frozen at some stage, and this is something to bear in mind when you purchase. Very occasionally live English prawns make an appearance at the market.

The two different groups of prawns are warm water prawns and cold water prawns from the North Atlantic. There are three main species of warm water prawn available for sale at the market; two types of white prawn and tiger prawn. These are imported from many different countries around the world from as far afield as Honduras, Brazil, India, Thailand, Madagascar and Vietnam (the list is extensive). The prawns are graded according to size and it is possible to buy a wide selection – generally the larger they are the more expensive. There are some sustainability and responsible sourcing issues surrounding warm water prawns and by-catch issues concerning those that are wild caught so there has been a fair amount of negative press over the years. Some of these issues have been addressed and many countries are now producing some excellent products.

Cold water prawns, harvested in the cold waters of the North Atlantic, are a real treat and something we enjoy working with at the school as they are so versatile. These are always sold cooked and frozen (both shell-on or peeled) on the market and can be purchased in various sizes, amounts and grades. The Canada Northern Prawn Fishery, which lands 68,000 tones annually, is Marine Stewardship Council certified.

In the freezer cabinets at the market there is a selection of ready-prepared and cooked prawns, so plenty to choose from. The flavour of shell-on prawns, peeled at home, is sweet and the meat succulent, really wonderful! At the school we use prawn shells for making stock (see page 183) and infusing oil – this is a great way of using as much of the product as possble and avoiding too much waste.

Lobster

There are two species of lobster available at the market. Around 75 per cent of sales of lobster at Billingsgate are wild caught lobster from Canada that are imported live into the UK. The remaining 25 per cent are native lobsters, caught from around the UK. Both are sold live but can be purchased cooked and they are a high value product. North American lobsters (many coming from Nova Scotia) are often slightly cheaper than the natives, although

FROM TOP TO BOTTOM: Cooked lobster, cooked cold water Atlantic prawns (in bowl), cooked brown crab, langoustines (bottom left), raw white prawns (bottom middle), raw tiger prawns (bottom right).

this will fluctuate at various times of the year. For the best quality many merchants would recommend native lobsters in the summer months and Canadian in the winter. Each merchant selling these will be able to show you the difference between the two. If you buy a live lobster and are unsure how to deal with it, ask the merchant when you make you purchase as they will give you tips. All the recipes in this book deal with cooked lobster.

Crab

Mainly live crabs and some whole cooked crabs, cooked crab claws, dressed crab in the shell and fresh and frozen prepared meat. The main species of crab on offer is the 'edible brown crab', which is harvested from British waters and the Channel Islands. Other crabs often available include imported blue coral crabs, velvet crabs and occasionally King crabs and spider crabs. White meat is the most popular and this is situated in the claws of the crab and the central body. Brown meat is tucked under the shell or the carapace of the crab. Males have bigger claws than females and therefore more white meat. Expect to pay more for a cock crab than a hen. Ask the merchant you are buying from and they will show you how to tell the difference. Brown edible crab caught in pots are considered to be sustainable. The advantage too is that they are alive when landed, so if they are too small (there is a minimum catch size for both crab and lobster) they can be returned to the sea to grow further.

If the crab is alive you will need to prepare it. It should be killed immediately before cooking. For the best way to do this, ask the merchant when buying the crab and they will give you advice. All recipes in this book use cooked crab. If you are buying a whole

cooked crab they are easy to prepare. For a simple step by step guide, see page 181. The meat of crab is white (found in the claws, legs and main body section) and brown (found in the carapace or main shell). White meat of a well cooked crab will be sweet and well-flavoured. Brown meat can vary in texture but has a much stronger flavour than the white meat, and some fishmongers add breadcrumbs and seasoning to this meat to make it firmer. For a simple dressed crab, wash the shell thoroughly and return the prepared meat to the shell, keeping the white and brown meat separate and serve with brown bread and butter.

Langoustine

Langoustine (or Dublin bay prawns, Norway lobster, scampi and nephrops) are on offer at several stands on the market. Sometimes they are packed on ice, but are occasionally sold live. They are highly prized and always fetch a good price. They are also extremely sought after in France and Spain and two thirds of langoustines landed in the UK end up being exported to the Continent. The flesh of a langoustine is sweet and succulent and it's well worth the effort of stripping them from their slightly tedious shells. The shells are also excellent for stock making. Most langoustine available at the market is sold raw, either fresh of frozen and some is breaded and sold as scampi. They have a delicate orange/pink coloured shell, which often leads people to the assumption that they are cooked, when they are not. There is a pigment in the shell of lobster and some prawns that is heat sensitive and turns red on cooking. Langoustine are naturally this colour when raw. They are simple to cook, requiring just 7–8 minutes in lightly salted boiling water.

Chilli Crab Linguini

Serves 2

3 tablespoons extra virgin olive oil
1 clove garlic, crushed
1 red chilli, seeded and chopped
250 g (9 oz) hand-picked white crab meat
1–2 tablespoons hand-picked brown crab meat
120 ml (4 fl oz) white wine
3 tablespoons finely chopped parsley
175 g (6 oz) fresh linguini
salt and freshly ground black pepper

Heat the olive oil in a large frying pan, add the crushed garlic and chilli and stir over the heat for 1 minute. Add the crab meat and stir until well combined. Add the wine, bring to the boil, season well and stir in the parsley.

Cook the linguini in boiling salted water until al dente, drain and toss with the crab mixture. Check the seasoning and serve immediately.

Seafood Crostini

Serves 2

1 small baguette, thinly sliced
splash of olive oil
1 clove garlic, halved
100 g (4 oz) cream cheese
25 g (1 oz) butter
1 tablespoon chopped chives, plus extra to garnish
150 g (5 oz) cooked North Atlantic prawns, peeled
50 g (2 oz) white crab meat
lemon juice, to taste
salt and freshly ground black pepper

Heat the oven to 190°C/375°F/gas mark 5.

Put the slices of baguette on a baking sheet, splash with olive oil and rub with the cut side of the garlic. Bake in the oven for 4–5 minutes or until lightly toasted. Leave to cool.

Meanwhile, put the cream cheese and butter in a food processor and whiz together until smooth. Add the chives, prawns and crab meat and pulse on and off until well combined but so that the prawns are not broken down too much. Add lemon juice and salt and pepper to taste.

Spoon the seafood mixture on top of the crostini and garnish with a few chives before serving.

Warm Tarragon Marinated
Prawn Salad

Serves 4

**20 peeled and deveined raw
  tiger prawns**
4 tablespoons chopped tarragon
grated zest and juice of 1 lime
**1 red chilli, seeded and finely
  chopped**
1 small clove garlic, crushed
4 tablespoons extra virgin olive oil
**salt and freshly ground black
  pepper**
**100 g (4 oz) sugar snap peas or
  mangetout**
**½ cucumber, seeded and sliced
  (leave skin on)**
1 celery stick, finely sliced
25 g (1 oz) dried cranberries
**50 g (2 oz) roasted and salted
  cashew nuts**

Butterfly the prawns and put them in a shallow dish. Mix together the tarragon, lime zest and juice, chilli, garlic and 3 tablespoons olive oil and season lightly with salt and pepper. Cover the prawns with clingfilm and marinate for 30 minutes.

Blanch the sugar snap peas or mangetout and toss together with the cucumber, celery and cranberries.

Heat the remaining olive oil in a large, nonstick frying pan, add the prawns and marinade and pan-fry for 1–2 minutes, turning the prawns until they are cooked through and are opaque and pink. Turn the prawns into the vegetables with any remaining pan juices and add the cashew nuts. Toss together and serve immediately.

Prawn & Samphire
Remoulade

Serves 4 (as a starter)

175 g (6 oz) samphire
450 g (1 lb) cooked North Atlantic
   prawns, peeled

FOR THE REMOULADE DRESSING
150 ml (5 fl oz) mayonnaise
5 tablespoons Greek yogurt
2 shallots, finely chopped
1 tablespoon chopped capers
1 tablespoon chopped gherkins
1 tablespoon chopped parsley
1 tablespoon chopped tarragon
1 tablespoon Dijon mustard
salt and freshly ground black
   pepper

Samphire is a delicious accompaniment to seafood and its salty flavour really cuts through the richness of this remoulade dressing.

Blanch the samphire in boiling water for 1 minute. Drain and rinse in cold water. Pat dry with absorbent kitchen paper.

Mix together the ingredients for the dressing and check the seasoning (you may not need extra salt). Fork in the prawns, add the samphire and pile into dishes to serve.

Pasta & Prawns
in Fennel & Pernod Butter
Serves 4

225 g (8 oz) dried penne
75 g (3 oz) butter
1 tablespoon Pernod
1 teaspoon fennel seeds
grated zest and juice of 1 lemon
1 kg (2¼ lb) cooked North Atlantic
    prawns, peeled
salt and freshly ground black
    pepper
3 tablespoons chopped chives

In a large saucepan cook the penne in boiling salted water until al dente. Drain and return to the saucepan.

In a separate pan melt the butter and heat until foaming. Add the Pernod, fennel seeds and lemon zest and cook for 1 minute. Stir in the prawns and lemon juice and season generously with salt and pepper.

Cook over a high heat for 1–2 minutes or until the prawns are piping hot and then toss into the pasta with the chives and serve immediately.

Langoustines

with Herby Fromage Frais Dressing

Serves 2

12 cooked langoustines

FOR THE DRESSING
large handful of basil
large handful of watercress
grated zest and juice of 1 lime,
 to taste
2 tablespoons mayonnaise
150 ml (5 fl oz) fromage frais

TO GARNISH
lemon wedges
flat leaf parsley

Arrange the langoustines on a large platter and garnish with lemon wedges and parsley.

Cook the basil and watercress in boiling water for 30 seconds. Rinse under cold water and pat dry with absorbent kitchen paper. Put in a food processor with the lime zest and juice and mayonnaise. Whiz together until well chopped and then add the fromage frais. Pulse the machine on and off to make a thoroughly mixed, bright green dressing. Spoon the dressing into a bowl to serve with the langoustines.

Creamy Seafood & Saffron Pasta

Serves 6 (as a starter)

750 g (1¾ lb) cooked North Atlantic
   prawns
1 small cooked lobster, meat
   removed from the shell
30 g (1¼ oz) butter
large pinch of cayenne pepper
1 teaspoon tomato purée
large pinch of saffron
1 small onion, finely chopped
1 celery stick, finely sliced
6 tablespoons white wine
2 sprigs of thyme
600 ml (1 pint) water
200 ml (7 fl oz) crème fraîche
300 g (11 oz) pappardelle pasta or
   linguini
salt and freshly ground black
   pepper
splash of lemon juice
3 tablespoons chopped flat leaf
   parsley

This rich and creamy pasta dish makes an excellent starter for a special dinner.

Peel the prawns and reserve both the prawn meat and shells. Dice the lobster meat and crush some of the shells.

Melt the butter in a large saucepan, add the cayenne pepper, tomato purée and saffron and fry over a medium heat for 1–2 minutes. Add the prawn and lobster shells, onion and celery and cook, stirring continuously, for a further 1–2 minutes.

Add the wine, thyme and water. Bring to the boil, reduce the heat and simmer for 20–25 minutes. Remove from the heat, strain and return to the saucepan, bring to the boil and simmer for a few minutes until the stock has reduced to about 200 ml (7 fl oz). Stir in the crème fraîche, bring to the boil and simmer for a few minutes until rich and creamy.

Meanwhile, cook the pasta according to the instructions on the packet until al dente. Drain and toss with the shellfish sauce, season to taste with salt, pepper and lemon juice and stir in the peeled prawns, lobster meat and parsley. Heat carefully until the seafood is piping hot and serve immediately.

Langoustines

with Lemon & Basil Dipping Butter

4–5 langoustines per person
lightly salted water

FOR THE DIPPING BUTTER
75 g (3 oz) butter
1 clove garlic, crushed
2 tablespoons shredded fresh basil
grated zest and juice of 1 small
 lemon
freshly ground black pepper

You should allow four or five langoustines for each diner in this dish, which can be adjusted to suit as many people as you like. The langoustines can be served warm or chilled.

Cook the langoustines in boiling salted water for 4–5 minutes or until the underside of each is opaque. Lift on to a plate and leave to cool and chill if you want to serve them cold.

Melt the butter in a saucepan, add the garlic and basil and cook over a low heat for 1–2 minutes to infuse. Remove and discard the garlic. Add the lemon zest and just enough juice to create a zingy flavoured dip, but do not make it too acidic. Season with pepper and serve with the langoustine.

Seafood Cocktail

Serves 4

450 g (1 lb) mixed frozen cooked
 seafood, including mussels,
 prawns, scallops and squid,
 defrosted
1 head cos (romaine) lettuce,
 washed and finely shredded
150 ml (5 fl oz) mayonnaise
5 tablespoons tomato chutney
1 tablespoon Worcestershire sauce
2 teaspoons creamed horseradish
Tabasco sauce, to taste
squeeze of lemon juice
paprika, to dust
salt and freshly ground black
 pepper

Season the seafood mix with pepper. Put the lettuce in 4 large, long-stemmed wine glasses. Sprinkle the seafood on top of the lettuce.

Mix together the mayonnaise, chutney, Worcestershire sauce, horseradish and Tabasco sauce. Season to taste with lemon juice and salt and pepper, then spoon sparingly over the prawns. Dust the top with a little paprika before serving.

Dressed Crab

Serves 2

675 g (1½ lb) cooked crab
oil, for brushing
2 tablespoons fresh white
** breadcrumbs**
salt and freshly ground black
** pepper**
French mustard (optional)
anchovy essence (optional)
cayenne pepper (optional)
Worcestershire sauce (optional)

TO GARNISH
1 hard-boiled egg, white chopped
** and yolk sieved (optional)**
chopped parsley (optional)

Remove the brown and white meat from the crab and set aside. Wash the shell well and brush with a little oil.

Mix the brown meat with enough breadcrumbs to allow them to bind. Season with salt and pepper or add mustard, anchovy essence, cayenne pepper or Worcestershire sauce to taste.

Pack both white and brown meat into the shell and garnish, if liked, with chopped hard-boiled egg white and sieved egg yolk and chopped parsley.

1 Twist off the claws and legs, crack the claws and carefully remove the meat.

2 Lever the main body of the crab from the carpace. Discard the gills and mouth piece.

3 Scoop the brown meat out of the carapace. Split the body shell in half and dig out white meat with the handle of a teaspoon or lobster pick. Scrub the carapace under cold water and press along the inner part of the shell to snap away along the natural line.

4 Clockwise from top left: brown meat (in bowl), gills, mouth and stomach (in bowl), cracked claw, legs, body shell, carapace.

1

2

3

4

Lobster Thermidor

Serves 2 (as a starter)

1 cooked Canadian lobster, about
  750 g (1¾ lb)

FOR THE SAUCE
50 g (2 oz) butter
2 shallots, finely chopped
½ teaspoon cayenne pepper
2 tablespoons brandy
1½ tablespoons plain flour
1 teaspoon French mustard
100 ml (3½ fl oz) dry white wine
150 ml (5 fl oz) seafood stock
  (see below)
8 tablespoons crème fraîche
1 tablespoon chopped tarragon
1 tablespoon chopped parsley
salt and freshly ground black
  pepper
2 tablespoon freshly grated
  Parmesan cheese

Prepare the lobster and split it open. Remove the digestive tract and stomach sac. Lift the meat from the tail end and cut into 2–3 pieces, replace in the tail of the lobster. Remove the bands from the claws and crack open. Lift the meat from the claws and arrange on top of the meat in the tail shell. Set aside.

Preheat the oven to 200°C/400°F/gas mark 6.

Melt the butter in a saucepan, add the shallots and cayenne pepper and stir over a low heat for 2–3 minutes. Heat and ignite the brandy and add to the shallots when the flames have died down. Stir in the flour and mustard. Cook over a low heat for 1–2 minutes. Blend in the wine and stock, bring to the boil, stirring continuously, and simmer for 2–3 minutes. Whisk in the crème fraîche and herbs and season to taste with salt and pepper.

Coat the lobster meat carefully with the sauce and sprinkle the top of each half of the lobster with Parmesan. Bake in the oven for 7–10 minutes or until hot and bubbling and the cheese has browned. Serve very hot.

Seafood Stock

1 tablespoon olive oil
1 small onion, chopped
1 small carrot, peeled and chopped
1 celery stick, thinly sliced
1 clove garlic, peeled
shells from 250 g (9 oz) raw tiger
  prawns
fish bones, skins and fins, preferably
  from white fish, such as plaice,
  sole, gurnard and sea bass
1 litre (1¾ pints) water
parsley stalks
1 bay leaf
1 sprig of thyme
black peppercorns

Take care when you are preparing the stock that you do not allow it to boil, which can make it cloudy. Do not cook the stock for more than 30 minutes or it may taste bitter.

Heat the oil in a large saucepan, add the vegetables and fry over a low heat until beginning to brown. Stir in the prawn shells and fry over a medium heat until they turn pink and begin to brown. Add the fish bones and fry over a high heat for 2–3 minutes. Pour over the water and bring to the boil. Reduce the heat so that the water gently bubbles. Add the herbs and peppercorns and cook over a low heat for 25 minutes.

Skim the stock with a large spoon at intervals. This prevents fat and impurities boiling into the liquid, which can impair the flavour and quality.

Remove from the heat and allow to stand for at least 15 minutes before straining and discarding the bones and vegetables.

Langoustines & Asparagus
Risotto

Serves 4

50 g (2 oz) butter
1 onion, finely chopped
2 cloves garlic, crushed
1 litre (1¾ pints) seafood stock
    (see page 183)
175 g (6 oz) arborio rice
1 glass of white wine
splash of extra virgin olive oil
12 langoustines, peeled and
    deveined, or 450 g (1 lb) raw tiger
    prawns
225 g (8 oz) small asparagus spears,
    blanched
2 teaspoons grated lemon zest
salt and freshly ground black
    pepper
flat leaf parsley, to garnish

Visitors to the school often admit some confusion over the names of this species of shellfish, sometimes known as langoustines, Dublin Bay prawns or nephrops. The peeled tails are also known as scampi.

Melt two-thirds of the butter in a large sauté pan. Stir in the onion, cover with a piece of dampened greaseproof paper and a lid. Cook over a low heat until soft and remove the paper. Stir in the garlic and cook for 2 minutes.

Put the stock in a saucepan, bring to a simmer and keep hot.

Tip the rice into the pan with the onion and stir for 1 minute to coat the grains. Add the wine and stir until it has evaporated.

Stir a ladleful of the hot stock into the rice. When the stock has been nearly absorbed, stir in another ladleful. Continue to add the stock, one ladleful at a time; this may take up to 25 minutes. When the rice is nearly cooked and all the stock has been added take the pan off the heat.

Meanwhile, blanch the langoustines in boiling water for 1 minutes. Drain and leave to cool for a few minutes, then peel. Season the langoustines lightly with salt and pepper. Heat the olive oil in a frying pan and add the langoustines. Stir-fry over a high heat for 30–60 seconds or until white in appearance and firm to the touch.

Add the asparagus and lemon zest to the risotto and season to taste with salt and pepper. Spoon into 4 warm bowls and dot with the remaining butter. Top each bowl with the langoustines, garnish with parsley and serve immediately.

Tempura
Seafood

Serves 4

16 tiger prawns, peeled and
   deveined
2 squid, prepared, scored and cut
   into strips (see page 39)
8 scallops, roe removed
100 g (4 oz) samphire, blanched

FOR THE BATTER
100 g (4 oz) plain flour
100 g (4 oz) cornflour
4 egg whites
300 ml (10 fl oz) sparkling water
pinch of salt

FOR THE DIPPING SAUCE
1 tablespoon sesame oil
2 tablespoons red wine vinegar
2 tablespoons soy sauce
3 tablespoons mirin
2 teaspoons pickled ginger, finely
   chopped
2 tablespoons clear honey

Heat a deep-fat fryer to 190°C (375°F). When the oil is nearly up to temperature, whisk together the ingredients for the batter.

Dip the seafood and samphire into the batter and deep-fry. The batter should be golden-brown and the seafood and samphire cooked through.

Make the dipping sauce by mixing together the ingredients in a small bowl.

Drain the seafood and samphire on absorbent kitchen paper and serve with the dipping sauce.

Squid, Cuttlefish & Octopus

What's on Offer

The cephalopod group of shellfish – squid, cuttlefish and octopus – are all available at the market and there are many products to choose from.

Squid

Squid is a hugely popular purchase and is available in a number of different forms. It is caught in every ocean around the globe and is quite possibly the most widely consumed seafood in the world. Fresh squid is available in a choice of sizes – small squid are perfect for stir-frying and larger squid can be used for stuffing and braising. Squid is also sold frozen and often ready-prepared as 'tubes', which can be purchased by the bag. Some merchants sell ready-to-cook squid rings in batter or breadcrumbs and squid is usually included as part of a frozen seafood mix. A fresh squid should have a pearly white flesh – as it loses condition the flesh turns pink. The membrane on the outside of the squid is delicate and comes away easily when jostled around in a box. It is simple to prepare – for instructions (see page 39).

Cuttlefish

Cuttlefish is popular with fishermen who use it as bait, but also with those who know just how fantastic it can be! Cuttlefish produces masses of ink that is gathered, pasteurized and sold in small 5 g sachets (some merchants sell these in small boxes). This ink is used in pasta-making and for colouring risotto nero to a deep inky black. The ink has a very mild taste but the colour is quite startling. Often the cuttlefish sold fresh at the market is covered in this ink. It needs similar preparation as squid: the tentacles should be removed and the eyes and beak (mouth) discarded. The internal shell is often seen at the bottom of a bird cage as it is excellent as a beak sharpener. The membrane should be peeled away. The tentacles need long slow cooking – quick cooking methods don't suit as the tentacles are prone to being quite tough. The head can be cut into very thin strips and stir-fried or added to a fish stew and they have a fabulous flavour. At the school it is often added to the Merchants Fish Stew recipe. It is slightly easier to cook than squid as it doesn't toughen so easily, but always use gloves to prepare it or expect to remain inky for a few days!

Octopus

Octopus is sold fresh and once purchased needs to be gutted and cleaned. The process is similar to squid, although there is no internal shell. On the market it is also sold frozen, which is excellent value for money. Some merchants sell it frozen in a ball – this is usually gutted and often tumbled in a machine prior to freezing, to help tenderize the flesh. Small octopus can be thinly sliced and stir-fried, but those with tentacles and bodies that are more than 1 cm (½ in) thick really benefit from long slow cooking. Most seafood is cooked very fast, but the cephalopods can be cooked for up to 2.5 hours. The Octopus in Balsamic Vinegar recipe demonstrates this slow cooking technique and the resulting dish is rich and the octopus meaty – a fantastic winter warmer.

Octopus
in Balsamic Vinegar

Serves 2

1 small octopus, about 450 g (1 lb)
8 shallots
4 cloves garlic
1 tablespoon olive oil
15 g (½ oz) butter
2 teaspoons brown sugar
3 tablespoons balsamic vinegar
300 ml (10 fl oz) dry white wine
300 ml (10 fl oz) seafood stock
   (see page 183)
4 sprigs of thyme, leaves only
salt and freshly ground black
   pepper

Try this with cuttlefish or squid

Preheat the oven to 150°C/300°F/gas mark 2.

Gut and rinse the octopus. Blanch the octopus in boiling water for 10 seconds, then lower into cold water, dip again in the boiling water and back into cold water. Do this 3–4 times; it will help tenderize the octopus. Cut the octopus head into 4 pieces and the tentacles into quarters.

Blanch the shallots in boiling water and peel away the skin. Trim away the hairy part of the root but leave the shallots whole. Peel the garlic cloves.

Heat the oil and butter together in an ovenproof casserole until the butter is beginning to brown. Add the whole octopus and brown for 2–3 minutes. Transfer to a plate. Add the shallots and garlic and cook for 2–3 minutes to allow to soften, stir in the sugar and cook until it begins to burn. Pour in the balsamic vinegar, wine and stock, bring to the boil and season lightly.

Replace the octopus and add the thyme leaves. Cover and cook in the oven for 2 hours or until the octopus is completely tender.

Remove the octopus, shallots and garlic and reduce the cooking liquid by boiling rapidly until it is syrupy in consistency. Slice the octopus and serve with the reduced sauce poured around it.

Braised Madras
Squid

Serves 4

2 tablespoons sunflower oil

1 large onion, finely chopped

2 small green chillies, seeded and finely chopped

2 cloves garlic, crushed

3 tablespoons spicy mango chutney

3 tablespoons mixed chopped herbs

300 g (11 oz) cooked couscous

8 small squid, prepared, tentacles reserved

3 tablespoons plain flour seasoned with salt, pepper and 1 tablespoon Madras curry spice

600 ml (1 pint) seafood stock (see page 183)

2–3 curry leaves (optional)

salt and freshly ground black pepper

TO SERVE

150 ml (5 fl oz) natural yogurt

¼ cucumber, peeled and diced

2 tablespoons chopped mint

Preheat the oven to 150°C/300°F/gas mark 2.

Heat 1 tablespoon oil in a small saucepan. Add the onion and chillies and cook over a low heat for 4–5 minutes or until soft. Add the garlic and continue to cook for a further minute. Stir in the chutney, chopped herbs and couscous, season to taste and leave to cool.

Score the outside of the squid tubes, taking care not to cut through to the centre of the squid. Fill the squid tubes with the couscous stuffing and secure the end of each with a cocktail stick. Carefully roll each squid tube in seasoned flour until well coated.

Heat the remaining oil in a large casserole, add the squid and fry for 1–2 minutes on all sides or until lightly browned. Pour over the stock, add the curry leaves (if used), cover and cook in the oven for 2 hours or until tender.

Lift the squid from the casserole and reduce the cooking liquid, if necessary, by boiling rapidly until syrupy in consistency.

Meanwhile, mix together the yogurt, cucumber and mint. Arrange the squid in a large dish, pour the reduced sauce over the top and serve the minted yogurt separately.

Salt & Pepper squid

Serves 4 (as a starter)

sunflower oil, for deep frying
2 squid, prepared, tentacles
    reserved
4 tablespoons cornflour
1 teaspoon each salt and freshly
ground black pepper

FOR THE DRESSING
1 tablespoon oil
1 teaspoon sesame oil
2 spring onions, finely sliced
1 clove garlic, finely sliced
1 red chilli, finely chopped
1 tablespoon dark soy sauce
splash of lime juice (to taste)
coriander leaves, to garnish

Preheat a deep-fat fryer to 170°C (340°F).

Open out the squid to form a flat sheet and score the outside carefully. Cut each into pieces. Toss together the cornflour and salt and pepper, then dip the squid into the mixture until evenly coated.

Deep-fry the squid for about 30 seconds or until golden-brown and just cooked through.

Meanwhile, make the dressing. Heat the oils together, add the spring onions, garlic and chilli and fry for 1–2 minutes or until just cooked. Remove from the heat and stir in the soy sauce and lime juice.

When the squid is cooked, spoon the dressing over the top and serve garnished with coriander leaves.

"I like fresh squid cut into strips and shallow fried, then served with salad, mayonnaise and an appropriately good white wine." **Don Tyler, J. Bennett Jnr.**

Exotic
Species

What's on Offer

Billingsgate market is unique not only for the diversity of fish species that are available, but also the diversity of different nationalities and cultures of the thousands of people that come and buy from the market each week. Saturday morning trading (as well as the periods around festivals: Christmas eve and Good Friday particularly) is renowned for being the big general public day and the market is so busy that it can take some time to even get into the market car park let alone find a parking space. We always recommend visitors on these days arrive in plenty of time. The aisles of the market hall are a heaving mass of enthusiastic buyers jostling for space to view the samples on offer. People are seeking out quality, but great value for money and the many species of fish that are not readily available in many of the large retailers. These buyers can be seen leaving the market with trolleys, cool boxes and shopping bags full of frozen and fresh fish.

Many come for the wide range of fresh and frozen exotic fish species bought in from the dozens of countries that export fish to the UK, and include a large variety of colourful snappers, beautiful parrot fish, rabbit fish, pomfret, groupers, barramundi, barracuda, scabbard fish and mahi mahi to name but a few – the list is quite extensive. This area of the market has grown over recent years and we often discover new species of fish making their first appearance.

Silver Scabbard

We sometimes use silver scabbard at the school. It is a long, snake-like fish measuring up to and over 2 metres (2 yards) long with a bright silver skin, big black eyes and a jaw full of very sharp teeth.

These fish are often line caught and are available as fresh and frozen (sometimes sold as ribbon fish) on the market. It is a very popular fish in Madeira and Portugal, where it is considered to be a delicacy. The fish is easy to prepare, just gut and cut into sections and grill. The flavour of this fish is almost butter-like.

Mahi Mahi

Mahi Mahi (or Dolphin fish – but no relation to the dolphin species) is another exotic fish that we occasionally use in the school. This fish is available whole and in vacuum packed fillets. It is quite a stunning fish, laterally compressed with a domed head and aqua, yellow and sea blue colourings. Fillet it for cooking and these are dense and meaty with an excellent flavour. This, along with tilapia, is used for recipes requiring exotic species.

Tilapia and Pangasius

Tilapia is another species of fish that is available in large quantities on the market both fresh, frozen, whole and filleted. It is farmed extensively in several countries around the world, including the UK, and this is considered to be a very sustainable method of harvesting. Other farmed species to look out for on the market is pangasius (or basa) fillets. In some cases these fish are fed a vegetarian diet and grow rapidly, too. Both of these fish are good value for money, low in fat and suit many methods of cooking. Tilapia in particular has a firm textured flesh and holds up very well to pan-frying. Pangasius is similar in texture and taste to plaice – so quite delicate.

FROM LEFT TO RIGHT: Yellow tail snapper and tilapia.

Vietnamese
Crispy Fish

Serves 4

1 tablespoon vegetable oil
4 cloves garlic, finely chopped
2 carrots, cut into thin batons
4 celery sticks, cut into thin batons
6 spring onions, finely sliced
4 tomatoes, seeds remove and
 roughly chopped
2 red bird's eye chillies, seeded and
 finely sliced
1 tablespoon palm sugar
2 tablespoons fish sauce
8 tablespoons water
oil, for frying
2 small exotic species of fish, such
 as talapia, heads removed, gutted
 and scaled, or mahi mahi steaks

TO GARNISH
coriander leaves
spring onions

Make the sauce. Heat the oil in a saucepan and add the garlic. Stir-fry for about 30 seconds, add the vegetables and chillies and cook for a further minute. Add the sugar, fish sauce and water and simmer until the sauce has become thick and pulpy. Set aside.

Preheat the oven to 200°C (400°F/gas mark 6). Heat a little oil in a large frying pan, add the fish and fry carefully on both sides for 2–3 minutes or until brown and crispy. Transfer to a baking sheet and finish cooking in the oven for a further 5–7 minutes.

Lift the fish on to a serving dish and pour the sauce over the top. Garnish with coriander and spring onions and serve immediately.

Escoveitch
Fish Salad

Serves 4

8 mahi mahi fillets
salt and freshly ground black
  pepper
grated zest of 1 lime
25 g (1 oz) plain flour
25 g (1 oz) fine polenta
2 teaspoon thyme leaves
5 tablespoons oil

FOR THE SAUCE
300 ml (10 fl oz) distilled malt
  vinegar
3 celery sticks, cut into matchsticks
1 carrot, peeled and cut into
  matchsticks
1 red onion, thinly sliced
1 red chilli, thinly sliced
1 tablespoon allspice berries
2 cloves garlic

FOR THE SALAD
handful of salad leaves
1 avocado, peeled, stoned and diced
150 g (5 oz) cherry tomatoes, halved
2 spring onions, finely sliced
oil, for drizzling

Escabeche is a traditional pickled fish dish originating from Spain, although it is probably more closely related now to the cuisine of Latin America. Escoveitch is a recipe along the same lines. Again it is a pickled fish dish, traditionally for mackerel, and it can be found on many Caribbean menus. This particular recipe is from Jamaica.

Skin and trim the fish fillets and season with salt and pepper. In a bowl mix together the lime zest, flour, polenta and thyme and roll the fish in this mixture until evenly coated.

Make the sauce. In a saucepan heat the vinegar with the celery, carrot, onion, chilli, allspice berries and garlic and simmer for 7–10 minutes or until the vegetables soften. Set aside.

Heat the oil in a large frying pan. Add the fish fillets and fry on both sides for 4–5 minutes or until the fish is cooked and the coating lightly golden. Lift on to absorbent kitchen paper to drain and arrange on a serving platter. Pour the escoveitch pickle and vegetables over the top and leave to marinate for a few hours.

Arrange the salad ingredients on a large platter and drizzle with a little oil. Arrange the fish on top and spoon over just enough of the pickle sauce and vegetables to moisten the dish. Serve immediately.

Try this with king fish

Steamed **Fish** with Wasabi & Ginger Marinade

Serves 4

4 white fish fillets, each 150–175 g (5–6 oz), skinned and pin-boned

This recipe uses several typical Japanese ingredients. The flavours work well with just about any fish or shellfish.

FOR THE WASABI MARINADE
2 cloves garlic, chopped
1 tablespoon pickled ginger
1 teaspoon sichuan peppercorns
1 teaspoon wasabi paste
1 tablespoon wakame flakes
2 tablespoons rice wine vinegar
1 tablespoon sunflower oil

Put the fish on a large plate. In a bowl mix together the ingredients for the marinade, pour over the fish, cover and refrigerate for 30 minutes.

Transfer the fish and marinade to a bamboo steamer. Place the steamer over a saucepan of simmering water and steam for 4–5 minutes or until the fish is cooked; it should be opaque and flaky.

Lift the fish on to a plate to serve, accompanied by Noodle Seaweed Salad (see below).

Noodle Seaweed **Salad**

Serves 4

225 g (8 oz) egg noodles (4 nests of dried egg noodles)
small handful of shiitake mushrooms, sliced
1 tablespoon sunflower oil
5 g (¼ oz) wakame flakes or nori seaweed

Cook the noodles in boiling water until tender, drain and set aside.

Cook the shiitake mushrooms in the oil and toss into the noodles along with the wakame flakes or seaweed. Allow to cool.

In a bowl mix together the ingredients for the dressing until well emulsified. Toss the dressing with the other ingredients and season to taste with extra soy sauce if necessary.

FOR THE DRESSING
4 tablespoons dark soy sauce
2 tablespoons sesame oil
2 tablespoons rice wine vinegar
2 teaspoons honey
½ cucumber, finely diced
2 celery sticks, finely sliced
2 spring onions, finely sliced
3 tablespoons chopped coriander

Roast Sesame
Fish

Serves 2

1 whole small fish, such as mullet or gurnard, scaled and cleaned

½ red chilli, seeded and finely chopped

1 teaspoon grated fresh root ginger

1 tablespoon olive oil

1 carrot and 1 celery stick, cut into very fine matchsticks (reserve trimmings for stock)

1 tablespoon roughly chopped coriander

large splash of soy sauce

small splash of sesame oil

1 teaspoon honey

2 teaspoons sesame seeds

freshly ground black pepper

Preheat the oven to 200°C (400°F/gas mark 6).

Slash the fish 3–4 times on each side. Put the fish on a large sheet of kitchen foil and sprinkle the remaining ingredients over the top. Roast in the oven for 12–15 minutes or until the fish is cooked and the seeds lightly toasted. Serve immediately.

"You can't beat a whole fish cooked in the oven – just really simple." **Rob & Ross, A. H. Cox**

Pan-fried Fish
with Achiote & Thyme Marinade

Serves 2

2 fish fillets, skin on

thyme or coriander leaves, to garnish

FOR THE MARINADE

2 cloves garlic, crushed

2 teaspoons thyme leaves

2 teaspoons achiote powder

1 teaspoon ground cumin

6 tablespoons sherry vinegar or red wine vinegar

salt and freshly ground black pepper

This combination of flavours works well with just about any fish, particularly oil-rich species such as tuna and exotic species such as king fish. Achiote is a spice that is used extensively in Latin American and Spanish cuisines.

Pin-bone the fish fillets if necessary and arrange in a large dish. Mix together the ingredients for the marinade and season lightly.

About 30 minutes before cooking the fish, pour the marinade over the fish and allow to marinate.

Preheat a nonstick griddle pan. Lift the fish from the marinade and griddle each side of the fillet for 2–3 minutes or until cooked. When the fish is nearly cooked pour over any remaining marinade, allow it to bubble up around the fish and then transfer the fish to a plate, pouring any cooking juices over the top. Garnish with herbs and serve immediately.

Beyond the
Market Hall

The market hall at Billingsgate is such a hive of activity that it seems hard to believe that so much else goes on besides the selling of fish. However, with such a large community of people working there, and so much to organise and arrange in order to keep the market running efficiently, it should come as no surprise that there's more to Billingsgate than fish trading.

Seafood Training School

As well as buying and selling fish, the ethos of Billingsgate is firmly entrenched in education. At a basic level this means trying to educate the public simply by introducing them to the wonderful array of fish on display at the stands. A visit to the market enables people to see so many varieties of fish and shellfish and, of course, to enjoy the whole market experience. However, for those who wish to take things further, The Seafood Training School offers a wealth of courses that cover a variety of topics and cater to everyone from kids, to food lovers, to professional chefs.

Set up as a charitable company by the Fishmongers' Company and the City of London, the aim of the school is to increase people's awareness of fish and to give them the skills and confidence to choose, prepare and cook their own fish. Fees from the adult training sessions are used to fund courses for school children free of charge. The philosophy of the school is to provide young people with the opportunity to learn more about fish in order to create a lifelong appreciation and taste for it. The school is located above the market hall, which affords it the ideal base from which to explore the market and learn more about different varieties of fish. Many of the courses begin with a market tour, during which fish is chosen for the subsequent demonstrations and recipes. This obviously means an early start for those attending but if you want the pick of the produce then you need to be up with the larks.

Escorted Market Visits

If you don't fancy filleting a fish at a time when you'd normally be tucking into your breakfast cereal you can still enjoy the market experience. Escorted market visits run throughout the year and involve small groups being shown around the market hall. Here, you'll get in-depth information on identifying and choosing fish, as well as the chance to chat to merchants and find out more about the day-to-day running of the market. Usually delivered by the training team or fisheries inspectors, the visit lasts about two hours and ends with a light and informal breakfast in the school. It's a great introduction to the market and, if you cook fish, you'll find the information indispensable.

Billingsgate Football Team

Although it has sadly been disbanded now, the Billingsgate Football Team was once the stuff of market legend. The team had a pretty good reputation and they used to practise and play matches at East Ham. They put up a good fight – sometimes literally, as well as metaphorically – against a number of police and local league sides over the years. The team is fondly remembered as a social activity that played a key role in creating a community feel at the market. Everyone turned out to watch the matches and support the team and it brought all the different areas of the market together.

One particular match went down in history and earned the team the name, 'The Magnificent Nine'. The story goes that Billingsgate were due to play the Post Office side in a key game that would see the Post Office win the league if they beat Billingsgate. Only nine members of the market team turned out for the match so the other side assumed victory before kick-off and were basically just going through the motions when the game began. However,

things didn't go according to plan and the Billingsgate boys managed an incredible 3-1 win. Needless to say, the celebrations at the market went on for some time.

The Market One-Mile Race

Another piece of Billingsgate folklore lives on to this day and that's the story of the famous Market Race. A local runner was in the porters' changing room one day when he set down a challenge. He claimed that he could beat anyone over one mile and he'd even give them a half lap lead. Buoyed on by the confidence in his running ability, he put down £20. This was an amount not to be sniffed it and it really set the challenge. Everyone knew he was fast but the chance to win some cash and wipe the smile off his face brought a few challengers out. The terms were agreed and two more porters joined the challenge.

One month later the four men met at the running track in Victoria Park in Hackney. A huge crowd had turned out to watch the, by now, infamous race and tensions were running high. When the challenge had been set, there was no mention as to whether the half lap would be taken from, or added to, the mile. A cunning merchant worked out that if he could run half a lap under the mile, he might stand a chance. So, he positioned the three Billingsgate men half a lap into the mile. That way, only the challenger was running the full mile. The mens' tactics involved running a fast first lap so they'd still appear to be ahead. Although risky, it paid off and the said merchant eventually came in to win the race by a couple of strides.

A Royal Visit

The market has seen many royal visits over the years and received some noble attention when His Royal Highness Prince William paid a visit in 2005. It was a great opportunity for Billingsgate to show off the sheer numbers and varieties of fish that are sold, as well as highlighting the importance of the market in terms of its historical and contemporary relevance. His Royal Highness took a tour of the market hall and stopped to chat to a number of the merchants. One can only assume that they took a rain check on their customarily liberal use of the English language. He was also shown the Seafood Training School where the Chief Inspector of the Fishmongers' Company was on hand to talk him through the facilities and the educational opportunities that the school offers. Public visits like this are obviously extremely important for Billingsgate as it brings the market to the attention of a much bigger audience. So many people aren't aware that the market is open to the general public. All publicity helps to keep the market in the spotlight and ensure that fish is given its rightful place on the menu.

The Lord Mayor of London

Each year the market receives a visit from the current Lord Mayor of London, accompanied by his sheriffs and the Mayor of Tower Hamlets. In keeping with tradition a fish is handed over by a merchant in lieu of ground rent.

Smoked

and Salted Fish

Smoked Fish

There are a handful of merchants on the market that specialize in smoked and or salted fish and there is always a surprising selection available. Both were initially methods of short and long term preservation in centuries past, but now they offer diversity in flavour and cooking.

Smoked Haddock

Haddock both fresh and smoked is one of the most popular fish at Billingsgate. At the old Billingsgate Market in the City of London there was a designated 'Haddock market', which proves its popularity.

Boxes of fresh whole haddocks and fillets are always available. Haddock is also the most popular white fish that is smoked. Up until the late 20th century Finnan Haddock (haddock smoked on the bone with skin on) was the most popular fish. Golden fillets of dyed haddock then became more popular, today it is the undyed fish that is the biggest seller.

Dyed haddock is experiencing a comeback and it is used in the school to add colour and vibrance to kedgeree as it is more visible. Some fish smokers have moved with the times and it is now possible to buy dyed smoked haddock that has been naturally coloured with the spice, turmeric and annatto, the colour used in red Leicester cheese – something to look out for.

Several companies sell smoked fish by the box and include many types of cold smoked haddock and hot smoked haddock in the form of traditional 'Arbroath Smokies'.

Both smoked cod and smoked cod's roe are also available. This is used for Taramasalata (see page 210) but the traditional fish used for this meza in Greece was smoked grey mullet roe. Icelandic smoked cod's roe is especially good. Icelandic is arguably considered the best to use, as the membrane surrounding the roe is thicker and more resilient and holds together better for smoking.

Smoked Salmon

Smoked salmon is a huge seller, too, and several merchants stock it. Available both cold and hot (or kiln roasted), it is packed and sold in quantities as little as 100 g (4 oz) right up to whole sides, d-cut and long sliced and in the case of kiln roasted, by the 3 kg (6.6 lb) box. Ready-packed organic, wild and branded smoked salmon (to name a few) from some of the best and most recognized producers can be found if you look around the market aisles. You will be able to buy some of the best in the UK.

Other products to be seen include smoked trout, smoked eel sold alongside pots of preserved salmon, lumpfish roe and other 'caviar types'.

Other Species of Smoked Fish

A variety of kippers (smoked herrings) from around the UK, including the MSC certified (and wonderful) Manx kippers, are widely considered to be the best in the UK. A wide variety of smoked mackerel (whole, fillets, peppered etc.), whole smoked sprats and various other smoked herrings including bloaters are also on sale.

Very little preparation is usually required, for vac-packed cold and hot smoked products to serve straight from the pack, it is advisable to open the pack about 30 minutes prior to serving to allow the fish to breathe. Other cold smoked fish need to be cooked and in the case of cold smoked haddock, poaching, baking and grilling are all recognized and popular methods.

Smoking will extend the shelf-life of a fish for a few days only. It does freeze well, so can be stored for longer periods of time in the freezer.

Salt Fish

A selection of salted fish is also available at the market including salt cod, salt pollack, salt ling and salt mackerel. Used extensively in the cuisines of Scandanavia, Portugal, Spain and the Caribbean, it is an excellent storecupboard ingredient as it has a long shelf life.

Salt cod is often sold as a whole, flattened fish, but strips of some, including pollack, are very easy to use.

The product needs to be soaked for at least 24 hours in several changes of water to rehydrate it and remove some of the salt. Blanching by dipping in boiling water can also help remove some of the salt. If not carefully prepared it can be salty, but this can be avoided if time is taken in the preparation. The texture of the fish is firmer, too, but it is excellent used in baked dishes and puréed in a classic dish such as brandade – the French salt cod and garlic purée.

Smoked Haddock

& Grainy Mustard Gratin   Serves 4

**450 g (1 lb) smoked haddock fillets,
  skinned (about 2 fillets)**
**300 ml (10 fl oz) half-fat crème
  fraîche**
2 tablespoons grainy mustard
2 tablespoons chopped parsley
**4 tablespoons grated mature
  Cheddar cheese**
4 tablespoons fresh breadcrumbs
**2 tablespoons grated Parmesan
  cheese**

TO SERVE
tagliatelle or long pasta

Preheat the oven to 190°C/375°F/gas mark 5. Pin-bone the haddock fillets, cut each into large pieces and arrange in an ovenproof gratin dish.

Mix together the crème fraîche, mustard, parsley and Cheddar. Spoon this mixture over the fish. Mix together the breadcrumbs and the Parmesan and sprinkle over the top of the fish. Bake for 12–15 minutes or until the fish is cooked and the topping is golden-brown. Serve with tagliatelle verde or other long noodle pasta.

Smoked Trout

& Salmon Dip   Serves 4 (as a starter)

4 hot-smoked trout fillets, skinned
**100 g (4 oz) smoked salmon, finely
  chopped**
500 ml (18 fl oz) fromage frais
creamed horseradish, to taste
lemon juice, to taste
2 tablespoons chopped chives
**salt and freshly ground black
  pepper**

TO SERVE
carrot and cucumber batons
melba toast

We make this recipe with smoked mackerel instead of trout and salmon for the school children who visit the school as part of our healthy-eating initiative and schools programme. We serve it with carrot, celery and cucumber batons and bread sticks, and the children love it.

Pin-bone the fish if necessary. Mash the smoked trout fillets with a fork and stir in the smoked salmon and fromage frais. Add creamed horseradish and lemon juice.

Stir in the chives and season to taste with salt and pepper. Serve with carrot and cucumber batons and melba toast.

Smoked Salmon Rarebit

Serves 4

175 g (6 oz) smoked salmon
4 thick slices of granary bread,
 toasted
2 egg yolks
5 tablespoons freshly grated
 mozzarella cheese
1 teaspoon Dijon mustard
1 tablespoon Worcestershire sauce
½ teaspoon anchovy essence
freshly ground black pepper
sprinkling of freshly grated
 Parmesan cheese

TO SERVE
lemon wedges

Preheat the grill to its highest setting.

Cut the salmon into thin shreds and arrange on top of the toasted bread. Mix together the egg yolks, mozzarella, mustard, Worcestershire sauce and anchovy essence and season lightly with pepper. Spoon over the smoked salmon and sprinkle with the Parmesan.

Grill for 2–3 minutes or until the top is golden-brown. Serve immediately with lemon wedges.

Taramasalata

Serves 4

2 slices of white bread
225 g (8 oz) smoked cod's roe,
 skinned
3 small cloves garlic
4 tablespoons sunflower oil
4 tablespoons olive oil
3 tablespoons Greek yogurt
juice of ½ lemon
freshly ground black pepper
carrot and celery sticks, to garnish

Traditionally made with smoked mullet roe, cod's roe is often used today. Icelandic cod's roe is particularly good and considered the best for smoking. The membrane surrounding the roe from fish caught in this cold water is slightly thicker and holds better during the smoking process.

Put all the ingredients in a food processor and whiz together to make a smooth paste.

Pile into a serving dish and serve garnished with the vegetable sticks.

Kedgeree

Serves 6

350 g (12 oz) basmati rice

½ teaspoon turmeric

350 g (12 oz) smoked fish, such as
   pollack or haddock, skinned

300 ml (10 fl oz) milk

75 g (3 oz) butter

2 teaspoons medium curry powder

1 teaspoon ground ginger or
   2 teaspoons grated fresh root
   ginger

1–2 red chillies (depending on taste),
   seeded and chopped

2 bunches of spring onions, finely
   sliced

salt and freshly ground black
   pepper

Try this with hot-smoked
salmon (kiln-roasted
salmon) or smoked
mackerel, neither of which
would require poaching first

After an early-morning market visit we often serve kedgeree for breakfast to those who join one of our full-day courses. It always goes down well and sets them up for the rest of the day. Traditionally kedgeree contains hard-boiled eggs, so these can be added if liked.

Cook the basmati in boiling salted water with the turmeric for 10–12 minutes or until tender. Drain and leave in a colander for a few minutes.

Cut the fish into 4 cm (1½ in) pieces and put them in a large saucepan. Pour over the milk and add enough cold water to cover the fish. Bring slowly to the boil, reduce the heat and poach for 3–4 minutes or until the fish is cooked and opaque. Drain away the liquid and set aside.

Melt the butter in a large saucepan or casserole and add the curry powder, ginger, chillies and spring onion. Stir over a medium heat for 3–4 minutes or until the onions are quite soft. Add the drained cooked rice and stir together until the whole is well mixed. Gently fork in the cooked fish, taking care not to break it up too much. Adjust the seasoning to taste and serve immediately.

Smoked Fish & Tomato
Bruschetta

Serves 4

4 thickly sliced bruschetta or baguettes
olive oil, to drizzle
225 g (8 oz) smoked fish, such as mackerel or haddock fillet, skinned and thinly sliced
8 cherry tomatoes, quartered
2 spring onions, finely sliced
1 tablespoon grated Cheddar cheese
1 tablespoon grated mozzarella cheese

This recipe is another favourite with the children who visit the school, few of whom would say no to fish pizza.

Preheat the oven to 220°C/400°F/gas mark 7.

Slice the bruschetta or cut the baguettes in half lengthways and drizzle with the olive oil. Arrange on a baking sheet.

Arrange 2 slices of fish on top of each baguette. Mix together the tomatoes and spring onions and spoon on top of the fish. Sprinkle with the cheese.

Bake in the oven for 7–8 minutes or until golden-brown and serve immediately.

Smoked Fish
Frittata

Serves 2

1 tablespoon olive oil
3 large flat mushrooms, thinly sliced
1 small courgette, thinly sliced
1 clove garlic, chopped
150 g (5 oz) smoked haddock, skinned and thickly sliced
3 large eggs, beaten
salt and freshly ground black pepper
pinch of freshly ground nutmeg
small handful of Parmesan shavings

Preheat the grill to its highest setting.

Heat the oil in a large, metal-handled frying pan, add the mushrooms and courgette and cook over a low heat until beginning to brown. Stir in the garlic and arrange the smoked haddock on top. Continue to cook for a further 2–3 minutes.

Pour the eggs over the vegetables and stir lightly to allow the egg to seep through the vegetables. Season with salt, pepper and nutmeg and cook over a low heat for 1–2 minutes or until the eggs are nearly set and the fish is just cooked. Sprinkle the Parmesan shavings over the top and finish under the grill. The frittata should be set and the cheese melted and golden-brown. Serve with rocket or watercress leaves.

TO SERVE
rocket or watercress leaves

Salt Fish Cakes

with Chilli Tomato

Makes 12

150 g (5 oz) salt fish fillets, soaked in several changes of cold water for 12 hours, preferably overnight
300 ml (10 fl oz) milk, for poaching
350 g (12 oz) cooked and mashed sweet potatoes
4 spring onions, finely sliced
grated zest of 1 lime
2 small red chillies, seeded and finely chopped
3 tablespoons chopped coriander
3 tablespoons plain flour seasoned with pepper
1 egg, beaten
handful of fresh white breadcrumbs
oil, for frying

FOR THE DRESSING
1 shallot, finely chopped
3 tomatoes, seeded and diced
1 red chilli, seeded and finely chopped
2 tablespoons roughly chopped flat leaf parsley
salt and freshly ground black pepper
lime juice, to taste
2 tablespoons extra virgin olive oil

Put the salt fish in a large frying pan with the milk and last change of water and cook over a low heat for 5–6 minutes or until the fish is cooked; it will flake away from the bone. Transfer to a plate, peel away the skin and remove any bones.

Mix the fish into the mashed sweet potato together with the spring onions, lime zest, chilli and coriander. Season generously with pepper only. Form the mixture into 12 balls and press flat; they should be about 2.5 cm (1 in) thick and about 6 cm (2½ in) across. Dust with seasoned flour, brush with egg and roll in the breadcrumbs. Chill for 15 minutes.

Make the dressing. Toss together the shallot, tomatoes, chilli and parsley and season lightly with salt and pepper. Dress with lime juice and olive oil.

Heat about 1 cm (½ in) oil in a large frying pan. Add the fish cakes and cook for 1–2 minutes on both sides or until the breadcrumbs are golden-brown. Transfer to a plate and pat dry with absorbent kitchen paper. Serve the fish cakes with the dressing spooned over the top.

Salt Pollack,
Chilli & Pepper Casserole   *Serves 4*

350 g (12 oz) salt pollack
4 tablespoons olive oil
2 teaspoons smoked paprika
2 onions, finely sliced
3 cloves garlic, chopped
2 red chillies, seeded and chopped
1 large baking potato, peeled and
    diced
2 red peppers, grilled, skins
    removed, seeded and sliced
410 g (14½ oz) can chopped
    tomatoes
1 tablespoon chopped parsley
1 tablespoon chopped thyme
freshly ground black pepper

Soak the fish in cold water for 24 hours. Change the water several times to extract as much salt as possible.

Preheat the oven to 180°C/350°F/gas mark 4.

Drain the fish and pat dry. Remove any skin or bones as necessary and cut the flesh into large flakes.

Heat the olive oil in a large, ovenproof casserole, add the paprika and onions and cook over a low heat until very soft. Add the garlic, chillies and potato and stir over a low heat for 2–3 minutes.

Stir the peppers, tomatoes and herbs into the casserole, season lightly with pepper, bring to the boil and simmer for 5 minutes. Add the fish and stir carefully to fold the fish into the mixture. Cover and bake in the oven for 20–25 minutes or until both the fish and potatoes are cooked. Serve straight from the casserole.

Kippers
Benedict

Serves 2

2 English muffins, split in half
2 kippers
6 tablespoons Greek yogurt or crème fraîche
2 egg yolks
2 teaspoons creamed horseradish
squeeze of lemon juice
1 tablespoon snipped chives
salt and freshly ground black pepper

TO SERVE
lemon wedges

Preheat the grill to its highest setting. Toast the muffins for a few seconds on each side until golden.

Meanwhile, put the kippers in a large metal bowl and pour enough boiling water from a kettle to cover. Leave to stand for 2 minutes.

Mix together the yogurt or crème fraîche, egg yolks and creamed horseradish, if using, and season with salt, pepper and a little lemon juice. Stir in the chives.

Lift the kippers from the water and pat dry. Fork away the flakes of fish, extracting as many bones as possible. Arrange the kipper fillets on top of the muffins and spoon the yogurt and egg mixture over the top.

Return to the grill and cook for 1–2 minutes or until the top is golden-brown. Serve with lemon wedges.

"We ate loads of kippers when I was a kid, kippers from a bag with butter. Don't know if you can still buy them like that but they were lovely." **Mark, Selsea**

INDEX

ACKNOWLEDGEMENTS

Although this book contains recipes I've written for school it could not have happened without some input from important people at the market. A huge thanks to Billingsgate Seafood Training School trustee and Chief Fisheries Inspector Chris Leftwich, who edited copy and offered his knowledge and insight into the species, buying and storing of fish. Thanks to The Market Committee of the City of London who oversee the running of the market and especially David Smith CBE, Director of Markets, and Malcolm MacLeod, the Superintendent of the market for their enthusiasm for the project. Importantly thanks to the London Fish Merchants Association (LFMA) and all the merchants and porters at the market who have willingly given their own thoughts and recipe tips (and who make my job such an enjoyable one); the team at the school who've contributed lots of thoughts and suggestions, including Adam Whittle, Terri McGeown, Phil Jolly, Rayner Moore and Iris Hindley; the Fisheries Inspectorate Barry O'Toole and Robert Embery, for all they contribute to our work at the school; Julian Cotterell Chairman and all the trustees of Billingagate Seafood Training School for their support for this project. I would also like to thank Cara Frost-Sharratt for her ability to observe the sprit of the market and to translate this into copy; Emma Pattison at New Holland Publishers for her enthusiasm, professionalism and understanding; food photographers Lis Parsons, for the technique shots, and Myles New for all his early morning efforts at the market and his ability to bring the place to life in a wonderful selection of reportage shots and also for his fabulous food shots; and a special thanks to Mick Mahoney for all his help in the techniques section and to New England Seafood for loaning him to us so willingly. The recipe testing and help with the food photography came from regular assistant chefs and trainers at the school, including Monaz Dumasia, Eithne Neame, Frances McKellar and Lori Poulton, to whom I am hugely grateful. Thanks to Tom Pickerell of the Shellfish Association of Great Britain, who gave us lots of advice on sustainability and responsible sourcing and who was very enthusiastic about the shellfish recipes! And last but not least thanks to all of the visitors to the school, past and present, and to my friends and family who helped to develop the recipes.